MORNING WILL COME

by
Sandy Day

MORNING WILL COME

by
Sandy Day

A book of hope and encouragement
for those who have suffered
the loss of a baby through miscarriage,
stillbirth, early infant death,
or are dealing with infertility.

*"Weeping may endure for a night,
but joy cometh in the morning."*
Psalm 30:5 (KJV)

MORNING WILL COME

by
Sandy Day

Unless otherwise noted, all Scripture is taken from
The New American Standard Bible
©1960, 1962, 1963, 1971, 1973, 1975, 1977, 1995
by The Lockman Foundation
Used by Permission

ISBN: 1-885904-48-7
Cover design by Barbara Richards

PRINTED IN THE UNITED STATES OF AMERICA
by Focus Publishing
Bemidji, Minnesota 56619

 DEDICATION

To all the babies represented in this book,
you have taught us so much
as Mommies and Daddies.

FOREWORD

"Dawn is about to break on us." Dr. Luke wrote this magnificent phrase in his inspired document and record of the Gospel describing the joy of the conception of Elizabeth's unborn son, and the ultimate meaning and eternal hope in the birth of Jesus Christ, the Son of God.

There is no greater expression of the character of God in marriage or in the perpetual evidence of the significance of man and woman than the desire and ability to procreate life. However, this dominant desire is too frequently delayed, postponed or withheld from hopeful couples. Only by trusting the prevailing fairness of the Creator, in whose discretion is life and death, can the pains of parting and new life be understood.

Our hearts are broken by many lesser things – but if in the anticipation of giving and receiving life – dreams are lost and our souls are hurt at the deepest levels, the comfort and sympathetic words and presence of others can embrace and empower us in the bonds of love. These knit together the raveled sleeve of care.

The precious, tender, yet strong experiences of the personal lives of those who have written in this volume, more than any clinical professional or documented information, meets the heart at its home. I personally, as pastor, friend, father and grandfather, have been humbled, touched and enriched by the power of these women and men to cope and to conquer.

It is with greatest joy that now their experiences can influence countless others to know that our "all-wise God does everything perfectly," and "no good will He ever withhold from those who walk uprightly."

Dr. Ross Rhoads
Charlotte, North Carolina

ACKNOWLEDGEMENTS

After 11 years of getting "Morning Will Come" into the hands of thousands of hurting women and couples, Focus Publishing has graciously decided to re-publish this precious book for us. MANY thanks to Jan Haley for her heart for ministry and her care for those who are hurting – you are priceless! I thank the Lord for Shelley who always answers the phone at Focus with love and compassion. Kimberly Malik spent countless hours editing, proofing, and giving wise counsel for all the stories as we were updating this book for publishing – you are a jewel! Thanks to Karen Cradit and Julie Teague for the time in proofing and your willingness at the end to help with all the stories. I have appreciated my dear friend, Nancy Fisher who always had a listening ear during this venture. I am thankful to ALL the women in Caleb Ministries and the Caleb Chapters for encouraging me to persevere with this project – God has blessed me with such a special staff of women. I would like to thank Dr. Lisa Hughes from the Charleston, South Carolina Caleb Chapter for her e-mail that got this whole book into the process of being re-published – WOW! Lastly, I could not have finished this project without my awesome husband, Craig. I always appreciate your steadfastness – you are our rock!

In the first printing from 1993, I would like to thank Amy Bristor and Patty Wade for all the many hours spent in typing, and for always being there for me in the wee hours. I could not have done this book without the two of you! Also, a special thank you to the many people who proofed and edited this very special book. Your giving of your talent and time was greatly appreciated. I would personally like to thank Martha Graham for writing the poem, "Morning Will Come" from Psalm 30:5, which has been used at countless baby graveside services and funerals.

TABLE OF CONTENTS

Appendix

INTRODUCTION

After the stillbirth of our son, Caleb, the Lord laid on my heart the need for a book which could share the personal stories of women who had been through "loss" and the process of recovery. The book would deal with infertility and crisis situations in the mother's pregnancy or the child's infancy. Three-and-a-half years later, at our first Caleb Cares meeting, (see Appendix), I asked if any of the women there would be willing to write their own stories to be included in such a book.

The outcome of that request is "Morning Will Come." These twelve stories (Jenny Dickinson's story added in this publication), though totally different and individual, have been placed under one of these three divisions:

Part I   Infertility and Miscarriage

Part II   Stillbirth

Part III Early Infant Death

The title, borrowed from the poem on the following page, was inspired by Psalm 30:5..."Weeping may endure for a night, but joy cometh in the morning."(KJV)

God is faithful. He understands our pain and walks with us through the night of darkness. He also instructs us to comfort one another. Sharing our pain and knowing that others have experienced similar traumas is an important part of healing. We pray that these stories will touch the lives of many hurting couples who desire children but have suffered disappointment in one way or another.

Sandy Day

MORNING WILL COME

by Martha Graham

Brokenhearted...
How can I bear the pain?
So many plans...permanently interrupted.
So many dreams...shattered.
Hopes...dashed.
All gone.
Why this?
Why us? Why me?
Helplessness...Hopelessness...
Life will never be the same again.
Is it even worth living?
Where are You, God?
I'm right here beside you, my child.
Even though you may not feel my presence,
I'm holding you close
under the shadow of my wings.
I will walk with you through this dark night.
Do not shrink from weeping.
I gave you tears for emotional release.
Don't try to hide your grief.
Let it become for you a source of healing,
a process of restoration,
for I have planned it so.
Those who mourn shall be blessed.
I'll be holding on to you,
even when you feel you can't hold on to Me.
Seek My face, child of Mine.
Receive My promise,
impossible as it may seem now,
that joy will come in the morning.
It may take much time, but I will heal your broken heart.
I know the night seems endless,
but MORNING WILL COME.
I have promised.

PART I
INFERTILITY &
MISCARRIAGE

"The Lord is near to the broken hearted, and saves those who are crushed in spirit." Psalm 34:18

IN HIS TIME

by Ann Foster

When we are surrendered to the Lord, our trials in life become opportunities for growth in grace. The beginning years of my married life were characterized by infertility, miscarriage and daily depression; but through the pain, Christ has brought me to a greater faith in Him and a burning desire to share His love and mercy with others.

As a child I spent many hours playing with my doll family, enjoying the feeling of responsibility and dreaming of the day when I would be a "real" mommy with lots of "real" babies!

Because of my own mother's terminal illness and early death, I was impressed by how fragile life can be and of the value of relationships with God, family, and friends. In high school, making friends and having a good time were top priorities, although I was careful to read my Bible and attend church. I didn't understand what the Bible meant by hardships and struggles and the growth that resulted. For me, living the Christian life was great! Perhaps the struggles were for the "non-Christians." When I graduated from college, my fairy tale would be complete by marrying Russell and starting our beautiful family. How comfortable life was; a home, traveling, church activities, and a wonderful husband. Of course God was my "disciplinarian", to keep me in line, but I had no concept of Him as my loving Father.

As our friends began to get pregnant, we too, decided that it was time to start our family. Certainly having a baby would be easy for us! As time passed, my desire to have a child became intense. What first began as an exciting possibility was fast becoming a frustrating challenge.

After a year of trying to conceive, we sought medical attention to determine if there was a problem. Russell and I underwent a series of tests— mine much more involved than his. I had blood tests, a dye injection test, and numerous pelvic examinations. My physician suggested that I have a laparoscopy to discover possible internal complications, which could be contributing to my severe cramping and heavy menstrual flow. I was petrified to have the surgery, fearing I could die from the anesthesia.

The morning of surgery, I felt helpless as they wheeled me away from my husband and mother-in-law. As I lay on the table, I prayed that the Lord would bring something good out of all this. I told Him that if it took this to have a baby, I was ready, but that I needed His help to get through it. Little did I know that my prayer would be answered in such a marvelous way. Infertility was to be my pathway into a Christ-filled life, based on total dependence and faith in the Lord.

Surgery revealed that I had endometriosis (a build-up of scar tissue), and a slight malformation of my uterus. My physician suggested major surgery to burn away the abnormal tissue. He felt we should wait to see if there were any miscarriages before dealing with the possible uterine malformation. He was very "matter-of-fact" with his information, and I felt as if I had been kicked in the stomach. I had a diagnosis of endometriosis and an improperly formed uterus. What was that? Why were all my friends getting pregnant with no problems and I had to deal with this? Why did God create me if I was not going to be able to bring a child into the world? After all, the reason I was here was to give my husband a child, wasn't it? I was confused, angry and felt defective, like a broken machine no one wanted anymore.

Russell and I sought spiritual answers to our questions. We read the Bible and listened intently in Sunday school and church for a clue. We were hurting and needed to hear of God's mercy and care. While searching for answers, the Lord led us to a Bible-centered church where God's love for us, His desire that we serve Him in all areas of our lives and seek His help for everything, was emphasized. We learned how He delights in giving us strength, guidance, and answers to prayer. The thought of God actually answering prayer was something new to us! We began to earnestly pray for a baby and to wait for His answer, whether it was "yes," "no," or "wait."

At the same time, we sought the opinion of a second doctor. He recommended further testing before undergoing the major surgery. We had new hope that perhaps one of these tests would do the trick. Although many of the tests were uncomfortable, both physically and emotionally, each test built our confidence that our infertility would be properly diagnosed, treated and cured. The doctor found my hormone level to be inadequate, so he prescribed Clomid, a fertility drug. Maybe God's handiwork needed a little earthly help, so I began taking the drug with much enthusiasm. Clomid gave me several side effects, the worst of which were sudden hot flashes. These became a family joke for they occurred at the most unlikely times—in the middle of the night (covers would fly!), in church, even during meals!

After several months on Clomid with no success, the doctor felt the laparoscopy would be necessary. Here I was, back in the hospital for the second time in a year, concerned and frightened, but trusting the Lord for a successful, safe surgery. How pleased I was to learn that the doctor had treated the endometriosis and done a procedure, which would lessen the severity of my monthly cramps. That was an unexpected blessing!

My recovery was slow, but I was filled with hope that the Lord was now ready to answer our prayers for a baby. (A word to the wise: don't ever think you have God's plan figured out. He works on His own schedule!)

Several months later I received the news that my father had died. My sense of loss was profound! Certainly I knew God was in control, but I felt so alone with both parents gone and no children to ease the hurt. Infertility had become an enormous burden to bear.

Imagine my excitement when exactly one month later, I conceived! It seemed God, in taking one life, was giving us another in answer to our prayers. His timing was remarkable and I was so excited!

After several blood tests, we were told of the possibility of twins. Being on fertility drugs increases the chances for multiple births. Twins sounded great to me. After three years of infertility, we were ready!

A week later I began to bleed, and although the lab work indicated that all was well, my doctor put me to bed. An early ultrasound showed there were two gestational sacs and one was deteriorating. Perhaps that was why I was bleeding – I was losing one of the babies. I lay in bed for ten days, awaiting another ultrasound.

During the second ultrasound, the nurses became quiet. Although I could tell nothing from the screen, I knew something was wrong. All too quickly I heard the devastating news – both sacs were empty – the babies were dead! We were heartbroken, having been through so much to get to this pregnancy.

Russell was with me and when I saw the look on his face, I knew he was hurting, not only for the loss of our babies, but for me as well. He was the one I depended on for strength and support and now he needed comfort. A husband's role in infertility can be extremely difficult.

We were faced with the decision to have a D&C (to surgically remove the dead tissue), or to wait for a spontaneous delivery. We decided on the surgery. This trip to the hospital was not one filled with hope for a diagnosis or treatment of a symptom, but one of despair—a wiping clean of the pregnancy I had dreamed of for so long. Again the question, "Why me?" I was confident this was the way of the Lord, but wondered what purpose all this pain and suffering had.

Afterwards, our next decision was to see an infertility specialist. It was so difficult each time I sat in the doctor's office waiting room filled with happy expectant mothers. I longed to carry around one of those swollen bellies. At the infertility clinic I saw women just like me, desperately wanting to conceive and have a completed pregnancy. I went through a series of new tests and began to feel like a science experiment with all the needles and equipment used on me. The specialist concluded that my ovulation was irregular and I would need to have blood drawn several times during my cycle to determine ovulation.

After working with us five months, he decided another laparoscopy was needed to further clear the endometriosis and to remove a growth (called a septum) on my uterus, which could create problems if an egg implanted there. After surgery he recommended a stronger fertility drug called Pergonal, requiring daily injections. Poor Russell patiently learned how to administer them, but never enjoyed causing me pain!

The drug put me on an emotional roller coaster of highs and lows. Excitement and hope the first two weeks of my cycle, impatience and sadness the second two weeks, and finally despair when my period came.

By the end of my second month on Pergonal, my period was late. Could this be another chance after five long years of waiting?

It was good news. I was thrilled, of course, yet used complete caution in telling only a handful of family and close friends. The infertility specialist monitored me closely. As my eighth week passed without complication, and an ultrasound showed a strong heartbeat from the baby, I returned to my regular obstetrician for the duration of the pregnancy. My husband and I had planned a trip to Disneyland the next week and both doctors saw no problem in our going.

Our trip was wonderful. I wanted to go up to everyone there and scream, "I'm pregnant! I'm going to bring life into this world. Praise the Lord!"

Russell drove back home and I stayed in California to attend a conference. One evening I began to bleed slightly and immediately called the doctor. He recommended bed rest. The next morning it seemed no better and I left for home, but by the time I saw the doctor the bleeding had stopped. I felt ridiculous, perhaps overreacting, but glad to be having another ultrasound.

As the ultrasound scanner went over my slightly swollen belly, that familiar silence filled the room once again. There was no heartbeat. Our ten-week-old baby had died, but was still intact in my uterus.

Tears overwhelmed us as we sat in the doctor's office, waiting for some kind of answer from him. What could he say? Lord, I wondered, what do you want from me— a broken spirit? Well, I'm broken! Still knowing this was all in God's plan, I wondered what it was that He wanted for us and just how much more pain the process would bring.

Further tests were performed, following the miscarriage. The doctor felt that the septum must still be intact and continued to be a problem, since the baby proved to be a perfectly healthy girl. Hearing the gender of our baby made losing her even more painful. I almost felt like a murderer and hated my defective body. Two weeks after having surgery to remove the septum, I began hemorrhaging and was returned to the hospital—to the maternity floor, no less! This time the surgery was successful and we were again able to pursue trying to get pregnant.

After eight months of unsuccessful attempts to conceive, we decided to take a break and put our energies into adopting. Until now I had only been interested in having my own biological child. However, time and pain had changed my outlook and I felt that having a child by adoption would be just as rewarding as giving birth to one. Anyway, I told the Lord I was open to anything!

Our series of interviews, references, family histories, views about life and child-rearing, feelings of having to prove our "worth" as suitable parents, became as emotionally exhausting as the infertility procedures had been. That year-and-a-half seemed endless.

It was at this time that I reached an all-time low. Knowing that one day we would get a phone call telling us we had a baby should have made me optimistic. Instead, I only felt depressed and couldn't pull myself out of it. We were told it could take another two years to get our phone call. We had already waited nearly seven years, two more seemed like an eternity.

For an entire week I searched my Bible day and night, asking the Lord for guidance. I also asked others to pray for us that we would know God's will. I desperately wanted to be free of the depression and of my constant tears, which left Russell wondering how to help.

Finally, one afternoon I sensed the Lord leading me to go back on the fertility drugs for one more month. That seemed unusual. It had been nearly a year since I'd even thought about the clinic and fertility drugs. But I was convinced that this was the Lord's will for me. I was surrounded with a feeling of complete peace and my depression lifted. That same week I was directed to read the Scripture in Luke 1:13b that says: **"...for your petition has been heard, and your wife Elizabeth will bear you a son, and you will give him the name John."** I marked the verse in my Bible and shared all this with Russell that evening. My enthusiasm convinced him that I had truly felt this was God's leading and not a crazy idea in my mind.

I picked up a thirty-day supply of fertility drugs, had blood drawn, and went home to gear up for another month of injections. About a week later, in the middle of the day, Russell walked through the front door. This was highly unusual and I could tell something was up. My first words were, "We don't have a baby do we?" He grinned and said, "Well, I sure wouldn't be home at this time of day for any other reason!" The caseworker had called Russell at work and given him the wonderful news that we had a baby boy waiting for us.

I was absolutely speechless. Our dream had finally come true. We had a son! A baby who would be ours! I could take him to the park, shopping, swimming, hiking, biking — everywhere and he would be **MINE**!

We had only a few hours that day to shop for everything we would need for the baby. My long list of things to do included a call to the clinic to find out how this would affect the workup we already had started. The doctor assured me that stopping the drugs would cause no problems. He added that he was thrilled to hear our wonderful news!

Our caseworker shared all she knew about our precious baby boy. We were especially touched by the unselfishness of his birth parents. It is impossible to express the gratitude we feel to them for this baby – the greatest gift we could ever receive.

Imagine our joy, the next day, as we flew to meet him. From our first glimpse of him lying there in a tiny bassinet, we felt an instant bond of love. I was almost afraid to touch him for fear this miracle was only a dream.

As Russell picked him up and handed him to me, the overwhelming love in my heart assured me that he was truly God's gift to us. My suffering had not been in vain and I was able to thank God for infertility, surgeries, and even pain. Here we were, "Parents," to this beautiful baby boy. What an awesome word!

The month following his arrival at home seemed like Christmas with all the phone calls, friends dropping by and beautiful gifts. My sister cross-stitched a verse we claimed for our son. **"For this boy I prayed, and the Lord has given me my petition which I asked of him" (1 Samuel 1:27).** There was that word "petition" again, just as the Lord had spoken in Luke 1.

The weeks passed quickly with so much to do. I joked with friends about only having twenty-four hours to prepare for motherhood, instead of the usual nine months. There was a lot to learn.

Very soon I became aware that my period was late and told myself that my "cycle" must be off due to all the excitement. Three days later, I went to the drug store to get a pregnancy test to confirm that I was <u>not</u> pregnant.

Imagine how odd I looked, holding a newborn and selecting a pregnancy test. The check out lady scolded me for even thinking I could be pregnant. I took the test home, followed the directions exactly, and was shocked to see the obvious "positive" results! That afternoon when I told Russell the news, he was speechless.

We now have three precious boys, each one chosen by God to arrive in His perfect time and unique way. Our love for these children cannot be measured and we feel privileged to have gone through the circumstances that led us to parenthood. I hope my story will bring you comfort, knowing that the Lord's timing is perfect and that He will see you through all the difficult times. I thank Him for all my past hurts for they have molded me into a stronger person, one who trusts in the Lord for all things and who has learned to wait for His time.

*"He hath made everything
beautiful in His time."* (NIV)
Ecclesiastes 3:11a

The Discovery Of A Calling

by Jenny Dickinson

I suppose many women and men try to imagine what their babies will look like once they are born. I used to try to imagine what I would look like pregnant. I must confess that when we started trying to conceive, I even stopped to look at maternity clothes in store windows. I could not wait to have the loose fitting wardrobe for my own.

That was nearly four years ago, the same time my husband and I set off for the adventure of our lives. He was to attend a three-year seminary in Oxford, England. I was thrilled! We both love to travel and could not wait to experience living abroad. We had been married about two years, so we also knew that we would start our family while we were in England. Since the day we were engaged, we often talked with anticipation and delight about becoming parents. Wouldn't I be cute, just like the other English "mums" with my pram and my rosy-cheeked baby playing in the pristine parks of Oxford!

In addition to starting a family, I planned to grow spiritually during our time in seminary. This was my chance before entering the ministry to be fed by God and to form a solid foundation upon which to start life as the wife of a minister. I was floating on clouds with elation, anticipation, and excitement! As I packed our suitcases, I marveled at what an amazing three years we would have! I could not wait to see the blessings that God was going to pour out into our lives. Things were going my way.

You have probably guessed by now that our plans for our seminary years did not unfold as we had imagined they would. I was fed by God, but my search for spiritual food came in the form of such intense despair that I could not bear another day, yet somehow I did. My faith grew by enduring suffering and grief as I walked through a deep valley of infertility before eventually coming out on the other side, rejoicing. I did become prepared for ministry, but for a very different kind of ministry. I can honestly say now, that if my plans for spiritual growth had transpired the way I originally thought they would, I would not be as prepared for ministry as I am now, and I would not be as close to God as I am today. It was through pain and sadness that I was drawn close to God.

As for my husband, he did train for ordination, pass his exams, and obtain a job at a wonderful church where we are happily serving. Thankfully, that part of the plan did work out for us! God did pour out His blessings upon us while we were in seminary, but they were not the ones we had expected.

After about a year of living in Oxford and "trying," we still had not conceived. I visited my doctor, and she said to give it another six months. The standard time in England before a diagnosis of infertility was one-and-a-half years. I was still a young and healthy twenty-eight year old, with a regular cycle, and my husband was healthy too. "It takes many couples more than a year to conceive," we were told.

So, we followed her advice. Six months later, still no baby. My highs and lows were becoming more defined, and they coincided with the beginning and end of my cycle. We lived and breathed by the calendar; month-to-month. After my cycle, I was excited and hopeful, "maybe this will be my month." Then each month, as disappointment set in, I would crash and enter a time of deep depression before the rollercoaster would start again.

People all over the place were getting pregnant. Every time an e-mail appeared in our inbox with the words, "Great News!," we knew it was another announcement of a baby-to-be from one of our friends back home. I felt like I was being tortured with each of those celebratory e-mails. Many of those messages were from long-time friends I love very much. I wanted to be happy for them; I wanted to rejoice with them. There were times that I suppose I was slightly happy for them, but most of the time I was not. Shocking? It seems so selfish to admit that I could not be happy for some of the people I love the most in this world, but I wanted to *be* them. Each time one of those e-mails came, I would crash again into a pit of sadness. The pattern was usually about three days of depression after hearing the announcement that someone was expecting.

In addition to the conceptions taking place back in the States, I joked that my husband's seminary was like living among rabbits. In England a pregnant woman's belly is called "a bump." Well, bumps abounded – they were everywhere! Tears had been constantly beneath the surface, but they began to flow at the sight of all those bumps and smiling ladies. It got to the point that I did not even want to go to the little crowded market where we did our grocery shopping. Inevitably there would be women with babies, and I would find myself getting mad at people I did not even know, because they had something that I so intensely wanted. My heart was hurting.

I started to think I was crazy. People, in an attempt to sympathize, would say things to me like: "No one is sick, no one is dying, this isn't such a big deal, just relax." They were right on some level. No one was sick, no one was dying, yet the hope of a new life created by my husband and me died each month I was not pregnant. A little person we thought would be with us was not. And I do believe it was a loss that needed grieving, a *VERY* significant loss! I have had the opportunity to talk to many women dealing with infertility, and the emotions are almost exactly the same in every case. The grief is just as profound and the despair is just as real as any other major life trauma. Something that is supposed to be so natural is not happening. It is important for women experiencing the loss of a hoped-for life to mourn that loss.

We began to seek medical help for our problem. After passing all the tests, our doctors were perplexed. Nothing was wrong with either of us. "You are still young," they said, "something will probably happen." Because of our schedule and the fact that we were spending the summer in America, we decided to give it a little more time. Following the advice of our doctors, we would pursue fertility treatment in the fall of our final seminary year if we did not conceive over the summer.

That summer was emotionally grueling for me. In my mind, this was the last chance at getting pregnant without any intervention, and the rollercoaster ride consisted of intense highs and crashing lows, all the while making me scream! Literally, screaming and yelling. One time I even threw a kitchen utensil at a wall so hard I bent it; this was anger, and it was real.

We began fertility treatments when we got back to Oxford. The first time we tried, it did not work. Once you enter into treatments, presumably your chances for getting pregnant increase and so do your hopes of quick results. It is impossible to describe with words the sadness and despair I felt after failed attempts at conception.

The other area that was becoming increasingly difficult for me was the anger. My fury had started previously, but, as time went on, I became more and more embittered. It was anger like I have never experienced and pray I never experience again. I was mad at everyone and everything. Most of all, I was mad at God. It may sound incredible coming from a minister's wife, but I told God regularly how furious I was with Him. How could He do this to me? Was I not doing enough for Him? I had followed my husband across an ocean into a life of ministry; not exactly the easiest of callings. We weren't going to make a large salary; didn't God know that fertility treatments were expensive (surely He did, He is God after all)? Why couldn't someone who had more financial security go through this instead of me? Didn't He care how much this hurt me? Didn't He care how depressed I was, how much anguish I was feeling each and every moment of each and every day? All this despair was exhausting; how could I go on one more day?

One day, I was talking to my husband about our struggles (by now this was becoming regular conversation in our household), and, as usual, I was angry. I told my husband (keep in mind, he is training for ministry) that I was not going to pray anymore. Why should I? It was doing me absolutely no good. If God was not going to answer my prayers, then why pray? God obviously did not care. I have often tended towards the dramatic, so I forcefully grabbed my Bible off of the table beside my bed and attempted to "storm" across the room and place the Bible on the bookshelf, where it would stay, unread. (Visualize a very tiny flat in England, smaller in total square feet than most people's living rooms: my dramatic "storm" across the room would have been much more effective in a larger room.) It really only took me about two steps to get that Bible on the shelf, and actually I could have reached the bookshelf from where I was sitting on the bed. But I wanted God to know I meant business! That is where it would stay until my prayers were answered!

My poor husband! Imagine what he was thinking! He would soon be interviewing for church jobs and would have to say, "No, my wife has given up on God and no longer prays or reads her Bible." What a team we would be, one person fresh out of seminary filled with enthusiasm about ministry and his relationship with God, and the other a bitter, angry wife. What a picture!

The struggle to start a family was very hard on him as well. There were several times when he wept to friends and mentors, despairing over what to do. But more than that, he was burdened because he could not fix it. Men always want to fix things, when most of the time, women just want to whine about things for a bit, and get some sympathy. We do not want a quick fix; we want someone to feel sorry for us. Well, I had been inconsolable for awhile now, and my husband was at the end of his rope. He could not help his wife, whom he loved so much, come out of that pit of sadness.

One section of the Bible that brought me great comfort (that is when the Bible was not relegated to the bookshelf) was from the book of Samuel. It is a story that is often quoted and read when dealing with infertility, but listen to the words describing Hannah when she was grieving over her childlessness. **"Whenever Hannah went up to the house of the Lord, her rival provoked her till she wept and would not eat. In bitterness of soul Hannah wept much and prayed to the Lord. And she made a vow saying, 'O Lord Almighty, if you will only look upon your servant's misery and remember me, and not forget your servant, but give her a son', ..And she kept on praying to the Lord. Hannah was praying in her heart. 'I am a woman who is deeply troubled. I have been pouring out my soul to the Lord, I have been praying here out of my anguish and grief'"** (I Samuel 1:7-18) (various).

Oh, how I identified with Hannah. Yes, this is from past times, and many things have changed since then. They did not use the word "infertility." They used the word "barren woman." Thank goodness we don't use that anymore! But the emotions that come when dealing with it are *exactly* the same: *wept, would not eat, bitterness of soul, wept much, look upon my misery, remember me, do not forget me, give me a baby, a woman who is deeply troubled, pouring out my soul, praying here out of my anguish and grief.* This was not a new problem. God has been listening to the prayers of women who desperately wanted to be mothers for thousands of years.

One day, I believe I hit rock bottom. A wonderful couple who lived in our building had a baby. I was friends with the woman, and she was perhaps the most sensitive to me during her pregnancy of any other pregnant person I knew. We had previously spent a good deal of time together, and she understood that it would not be possible for me to spend as much time with her now that she was expecting. I am forever grateful to her for this sensitivity. Quite often, people were not sensitive, and that is so important when dealing with friends who are struggling with infertility. If she ever comes across this story, I would not want her to feel guilty or sad. She is a wonderful woman of God, and I am thankful for the unspoken way she ministered to me during her pregnancy and early days of motherhood.

Nonetheless, it was the day they brought their beautiful baby home from the hospital that I journeyed to the absolute depth of my pain. I used to think that it was a mistake for me to have stayed home that day, but I believe God put me there so I would hit rock bottom. It was necessary for me to hit the bottom so I could surrender and move, finally, out of a place of suffering.

We lived in a building of eight tiny flats with a common front door. Our flat was on the front of the building, on the top floor, overlooking the entryway and parking lot. It was a beautiful sunny day. People started coming bearing balloons, casseroles, and flowers. A few times people rang our doorbell because the doorbell of this couple's flat was broken.

More than once, I walked all the way down to the bottom floor to let in the smiling faces and gifts that welcomed this baby into the world.

That was supposed to be *me*! We had been trying for a baby for so long! Crying was becoming the norm for me, but I wept that day more than I have ever wept at one time. It was also a weeping that came from the depths of my soul, just like Hannah. I could not stop. I called my husband who was down the road at the college working on an essay. He came home and held me for awhile. I did not stop weeping. Finally, he went back to his study – there was nothing else he could do – it was just God and me, in a stand-off.

I do not really remember how that day ended. I think I was so exhausted by the time I finally stopped crying that I got in the bed and went to sleep. The bigger ending to that day is that I let go of my pain, because I simply could not bear it anymore. I finally allowed God to lead me down the path *He* had for me. I relinquished myself to His will and stopped fighting for my own. I pulled the Bible down from the shelf and gave it a good dusting. God won the standoff.

I now see that even during the three years I was struggling with infertility, God was slowly placing the desire to adopt upon my heart. It is impossible to put this into words. He did not write anything in the sky, I just knew it in my heart. He wanted us to adopt. Perhaps, one day, I would be pregnant. But right now, He wanted us to adopt. It was the first time I understood the notion of a "calling." My husband had experienced this when he discovered that God was calling him to be a minister. Shortly after the day I hit rock bottom, the calling to adopt became so strong, that I knew I had to do it. In fact, doing anything else, and that included continuing with fertility treatments, would be going against God's will for us. He had slowly transformed my heart according to His will.

We had only a few more months left in England after "Rock Bottom Day," and they were glorious. While our three years there were filled with deep sadness, there was also abundant joy. We had been blessed with some of the most amazing friends in the world. Two in particular come to mind. They were my best girlfriends, and I will never forget how they stood by me through the most difficult time in my life. What I went through was awful, but if I had to go through that to form these two very special friendships, it was worth it. They prayed for me and spent time with me when I was not the most pleasant person. They continue to pray for the baby that is waiting to join our family, and they are perhaps the two most excited people (except the grandmothers-to-be) about our adoption. When you have friends who empathize so much that they shed their own tears for you, you are blessed beyond all imagination. Even though we had many hard days, we cherished our living abroad experience and had grown so close as husband and wife. We loved our life in England and are still homesick for that very special place.

God's blessings continued to pour out on us as we left Oxford. We were sent to a great church in Charleston, South Carolina, and the love and warmth we felt immediately was overwhelming.

Since moving back to the States, I have participated in hosting several baby showers for expectant friends. One year ago, I would not have been able to give that shower. I could not even look at a pregnant woman without bursting into tears, much less sit by and watch one open packages containing tiny clothes. Giving these showers has been one of the most joyful experiences of my life. One reason is because they are being given for such special people. They treat my planned adoption as equally exciting as their pregnancies. This has been a true blessing, and I thank God for them every day.

The other, perhaps more poignant, reason this has been such a joyful experience for me is that I finally feel free from the enormous weight infertility placed upon me. I am able to be truly happy for these women and am sincerely excited about meeting their precious children. Not one part of me is jealous, angry, or bitter. I wanted to be happy for all of those pregnant people I knew and loved in the past, but the bitterness was keeping me from true joy. I am so glad that my soul can genuinely be happy for others who are awaiting the gift of children. The freedom is amazing!

One of the verses I wrote in my journal during our struggles with infertility was from **Psalm 16:5-6: "Lord, you have assigned me my portion and my cup; you have made my lot secure. The boundary lines have fallen for me in pleasant places; surely I have a delightful inheritance."**

I copied down that verse at a time when I probably did not believe it, but oh how it speaks to me now! My lot is secure! There is no doubt in my mind that this is what I am meant to do at this time. It makes me shudder to think that had I persisted in my own stubbornness, I would not have known the pleasure of being in God's will by pursuing adoption.

About the middle of our three-year struggle with infertility, I wrote the following verses from Psalm 13 in my journal:

"How long, O Lord? Will you forget me forever? How long will you hide your face from me? How long must I wrestle with my thoughts and every day have sorrow in my heart?...Look on me and answer, O Lord my God. But I trust in your unfailing love; my heart rejoices in Your salvation. I will sing to the Lord, for He has been good to me."

The first part of that verse describes me during those trying three years we struggled with childlessness. The last part describes me now – trusting in God's unfailing love and rejoicing, singing to the Lord, for He has been good to me. How did I get to that place? By finally surrendering myself to God and His perfect plan. I had no choice; I could not continue the way of depression, fear, and anger. Yes, it was a choice I made, but it was also God lifting me out of the depths.

So I did grow spiritually during our seminary years. At times, I did not realize I was growing spiritually, because I was not even speaking to God. But if I had not gone through a time of suffering, I would not be able to trust God as I do now. Just as He placed the desire in my heart to be a mother, so has He placed the desire in my heart to become a mother by adopting a baby.

So why did I go through this experience? I cannot fully answer that now. As my mother said when I told her I would be writing this story, "But you don't know the ending yet!" But I believe when I first see my baby's face, it will make perfect sense. I think this verse from my journal says it best:

"I am still confident of this: I will see the goodness of the Lord in the land of the living. Wait for the Lord; be strong and take heart and wait for the Lord" (Psalm 27:13-14).

MY GOD
OF THE VALLEYS

by Shirley Gray

Tony and I became Christians as teenagers, so when we were married, we were excited about establishing a Christ-centered home and starting our lives together as husband and wife. We were like most couples who look forward to traveling, establishing careers, buying a home and starting a family.

We came to Charlotte, North Carolina, and the Lord led us to a wonderful, gospel-preaching church where we began to make Christian friends and grow in the Lord. As time went by, we met several couples that had been trying unsuccessfully to have children. We also met couples that had lost children through miscarriage. I had a real burden for these couples, and we began to pray for them to be blessed with children. I tried to understand what they must be experiencing even though Tony and I weren't ready to start our family yet. As we continued to pray diligently for these couples, little did we know that through their experiences, God was preparing us for trials ahead in our own lives.

Eventually we began to talk about our growing desire to have children. We tried for several months, unsuccessfully, to conceive and neither of us really thought much about it. I became more concerned after six months of trying. I kept thinking about our friends who had tried for years to have children. All the while, this desire in us grew stronger and stronger. After a year, Tony and I both agreed that perhaps it would be a good idea to see a doctor since I had not yet become pregnant.

I called my doctor and made an appointment. He examined me and ran several blood tests to look for hormonal imbalances, and requested that my husband have some tests run too. He asked me to begin using a basal temperature chart. This meant that I would take my temperature each morning before getting out of bed and record it on a graph. He explained that when my temperature went up, I would ovulate within the next 24-48 hours. He also explained that the chart would show if my cycle was normal and if I was ovulating. He instructed me to do this for three months and, if I still was not pregnant, to see him again.

I began to follow the doctor's instructions, feeling confident that now we would surely conceive. Tony and I prayed that the Lord would bless us with a child, confidently trusting that He would.

Our blood tests showed no abnormalities. We both were encouraged that so far nothing physically was found to be wrong with either of us. I diligently took my temperature every morning, recorded it on the graph, and watched for it to begin to rise. When my temperature went up so did our hopes. Would this be the month that I would become pregnant? Each month we would be disappointed once again. This was to be the beginning of many months of waking up to place a thermometer in my mouth. It was also the onset of a monthly, emotional roller coaster ride; beginning with great hope and anticipation, and plunging to deep disappointment and depression when no baby was conceived.

As time went by, we gradually began to share with some Christian friends our deepest, most personal prayer request. This was not something we felt we could discuss easily with others, but the Lord had given us some very caring and compassionate friends. It was a great consolation to know that others were holding us up in prayer.

I desperately needed patience during these months of waiting. I was becoming more and more frustrated with God, and with why He had not answered our prayers for a child. One day as I was studying His Word, He opened my eyes to Isaiah 40:31: **"Yet those who wait for the Lord will gain new strength; they will mount up with wings like eagles, they will run and not get tired, they will walk and not become weary."**

I knew that this verse was for me. Through it, God gave me a renewed strength to go on, and a challenge to wait patiently for Him. We placed our complete trust in Him to give us the child we so greatly desired.

Tony and I had traveled down this difficult path for little more than a year, but already it seemed like an eternity. With each passing month, the desire to have a child grew stronger and burned more deeply in my heart. I had always thought it would be easy to get pregnant, and decided spring would be a nice time to have a baby. Now it didn't matter about the timing, as long as everything was safe. I could see my previous thoughts had been so trivial.

My relationship with Tony grew even stronger in the midst of all the disappointment. He was so comforting and uplifting, although I knew he was longing for a child as much as I. He faced the same disappointments, and yet was trying very hard to understand my emotions and to always be supportive.

Three months of temperature-taking went by, and I did not become pregnant. I found myself constantly looking at a calendar and counting 28 days. It was as if my life revolved around a calendar. Some days I felt consumed by the emotional ups and downs brought by this constant awareness of time.

I made an appointment and returned to see my doctor with temperature charts in hand. He looked at them and found no significant problem. I was almost in tears, feeling fearful of what step to take next. He prescribed a fertility drug called Clomid that would help me to produce more eggs each month. This would increase my chances of getting pregnant.

Once again I was encouraged, feeling that this was the answer we had waited for. The Lord would surely give us a child now.

Indeed, I became pregnant during the second month of taking Clomid. The day I found out the good news, I could hardly wait to get home to tell Tony. We both knew this had to be the Lord's perfect timing. Everything seemed so much in order. We had bought a home. We both were established in our jobs. Tony had just become a registered architect. It was perfect! As a precaution, we waited until I was about eight weeks pregnant to tell anyone. It was so exciting to share our long-awaited good news with friends and family.

At work, there was a group of women who were pregnant. We had fun comparing notes with each other as our pregnancies progressed.

Our baby was due on June 10th. Tony and I prayed that the Lord would care for and protect this child throughout the pregnancy. From the very first day we learned of his existence, we dedicated him to the Lord. Our hearts were truly thankful for this answered prayer and for God's blessing in our lives.

Fourteen weeks into my pregnancy, I awoke on Sunday morning and found that I was spotting. I immediately became frightened, fearing the worst and prayed, "God, please don't let me lose this baby." I had so many questions running through my mind. I prayed for God's strength to get me through this fearful time and His protection for our child. I kept thinking, "I'm supposed to be out of danger of miscarriage. I'm out of the first trimester. Why is this happening to us?" Then I thought, "Maybe this kind of spotting is normal. I'll just call the doctor and he will tell me everything is okay and not to worry." Tony sat next to me, holding my hand, as I phoned my doctor. He wanted us to meet him at the hospital for an ultrasound to make sure everything was all right.

We were only ten minutes from the hospital. As we drove, I held Tony's hand tightly and prayed all the way. When we arrived, a nurse took us into a small examination room where we anxiously awaited the doctor's arrival. He came in and asked a few questions in a very compassionate manner. Then the nurse turned off the lights so he could see the ultrasound screen. As he looked at that small screen for what seemed an eternity, silence filled the room. Out of the corner of my eye, I saw the nurse reach for a box of tissues. The doctor looked up and said, "I'm sorry. There is no heartbeat. This baby has not developed now for several weeks." I just looked at him in shock, and then I looked at the ultrasound screen. Tears began to fill my eyes and roll down my face. He further explained that our baby had probably died several weeks earlier and that my body had just not responded yet. I could not believe this was happening to us. I thought that surely since we had experienced so much difficulty conceiving a child, that the Lord wouldn't take one from us now!

The doctor came back to talk with us again, showing sympathetic understanding of our grief. He explained that the next step was a D&C. As I was being prepped for the surgery, I can remember in my mind questioning God, questioning the doctor. Was our baby really dead? Why did this happen? Then I remembered the picture on the ultrasound screen. There was no movement. There was not even a little flicker of light indicating a heartbeat. There was no life.

As we drove home after the surgery, though still groggy from the anesthesia, I felt very empty inside. Our baby that we had prayed for and planned for was gone. It seemed so unfair. That night, as the effects of the anesthesia wore off, Tony came into the bedroom and we embraced. Holding each other tightly we sobbed, grieving the loss of our precious child.

As I awoke the next morning, a flood of tears came again. I felt out of control and helpless. I knew I needed God now more than I had ever needed Him. My faith was weak. For several days, I could not find the words to pray and could not even pick up my Bible. Then I prayed, "Lord, I know I can't get through this on my own. I need You." I picked up my Bible and read the Twenty-Third Psalm. For the first time in my life, I understood what it meant to walk through the valley of the shadow of death. I had never experienced pain like this or such loss. God seemed very far away. I wanted instant relief from this hurt. At times guilty feelings that perhaps I had done something to cause the miscarriage overwhelmed me.

I felt a strong need to talk with others about the loss of our child. The Lord was faithful, and sent those friends to me for whom we had prayed. These women understood what it was like to go through similar hurt and were a tremendous comfort to me.

It was difficult for me to go back to work the next week and face people who would not know what to say to me. I was still very emotional. I knew that every time someone spoke to me, a wave of tears would come. It was so hard to deal with comments from those with good intentions like: "You're young, you can have another baby", "Your baby is better off now," "This is God's way of taking care of a problem," "Your baby is in a better place." I did not draw comfort from remarks like these. I wanted THAT baby! Being with the group of women at work who were pregnant was the hardest of all. I was now on the outside looking in. They had their babies and mine was gone. I felt envious of them. I wondered why I had to be another statistic. Why did I have to be the one who lost my baby? I did not wish this hurt on anyone, but I did not want it for myself either.

The next few weeks were difficult. I went through the motions of finishing Christmas shopping and going to parties although a large void filled my heart. Even family members did not know what to say to me. While I needed to talk about the death of our baby, it seemed to make most people uncomfortable.

Christmas Day was the worst. I cried frequently and felt very unstable. I knew our baby was in Heaven in Jesus' arms, but I wanted to hold him. I wanted to feel him move in my womb. I wanted to hear his first cry. I felt so robbed that his life had been taken from Tony and me so suddenly. I began to feel angry at God for allowing this to happen to us. How my heart ached for this child.

As the weeks went by, I had daily fluctuations of emotions. I tried to get on with my life. I turned to God's Word more often than I ever had before; I prayed more often than I ever had before. I knew I needed the "God of all comfort" as I had never needed Him before. This was only the beginning of times when I would need my Good Shepherd to pick me up and carry me through the dark and painful valleys.

After two months, we were able to try to conceive again. I went back on the medication and again began taking my temperature. I found myself once more on the emotional roller coaster of a 28-day cycle. This continued for five more months. Even after increasing the dosage of Clomid, we still were unable to conceive. My frustration bordered on panic. There were days when my desire for a baby simply overwhelmed me. I tried to be happy and upbeat. Wasn't this the image that Christians should project? I found myself hiding my depression and sadness, and feeling guilty when I was unhappy. I certainly didn't feel like smiling all the time. After all, I had a right to grieve.

My emotions were on edge as June 10th approached. This was our baby's due date. I had thought I would be pregnant again by now. I had dreamed of getting the nursery ready and bringing our little bundle home. But there was no little bundle.

I clearly remember sitting in Sunday School with Tony just prior to that date. The well-intentioned teacher in our class asked all the pregnant women to raise their hands so our class could pray for them and their babies. As they raised their hands my heart sank. They couldn't have realized how brokenhearted I felt as I was reminded again of my loss. Those old wounds were once again reopened. I felt the tears coming, and could only look down at the floor. Tony was so perceptive and knowingly reached over and gave my hand a tight squeeze. All I could think was, "I'm supposed to be pregnant! Why did this happen to me?"

About one month later, my father died. He had been seriously ill for several months, and I found myself experiencing yet another loss and more emptiness. The grieving started all over again. I was terribly saddened that I had been unable to give my father a grandchild before he died. I now felt even more desperate to have a child. This desperation caused me to consider taking another step. Should I see an infertility specialist?

We had been trying unsuccessfully to conceive for six months since my miscarriage. I was torn as to whether to trust God totally for a child without further medical intervention, or whether to take a more aggressive approach and see a specialist. Would it be a lack of faith for me to seek help? I knew that God could work through physicians and medicine, but what did He want me to do? I also struggled with the impact of being labeled "infertile," although that is what I was. Tony and I prayed for the Lord's guidance in our situation. I knew that Tony would be supportive of me no matter what decision I made.

Several weeks went by, and I felt the Lord leading me to call an old friend who had been through extensive infertility testing and several miscarriages. As we met and discussed my situation, she told me of a reproductive endocrinologist who had helped her. She now had a wonderful little boy. She encouraged me to go home and make an appointment. She was very emphatic about not having time to waste as we get older. I believed this was my answer from God through this dear friend. I went home and made the appointment.

At my first visit the specialist asked many detailed questions and ran some extensive tests. About two weeks later, he informed me of my diagnosis – Polycystic Ovarian Disorder. I had never heard of it. I was thankful that finally there was a diagnosis, and that we were on the road to treating it. He explained to me that I was ovulating each month, but that the eggs I was producing were small, immature and poorly-developed. He told us that this is a fairly common disorder, and that it could be treated with fertility drugs. After further testing with Clomid, the medication I had taken previously, he discovered that my body was reacting adversely to it, causing the sperm to die before ever reaching the egg. I was very encouraged that already in a short amount of time, he had found two problems, both of which he felt were very treatable. I felt strongly now that we had made the right decision in coming to see him, and that yes, the Lord could work through physicians and modern medicine.

The next step was a big one. He recommended that I go on a more powerful fertility drug called Metrodin. This drug was given by intra-muscular injection in the evening for about five to seven days prior to ovulation to stimulate the ovaries. This would help my body produce a greater number of healthy eggs and would greatly increase my chances of getting pregnant. It would also mean frequent visits to the doctor's office for ultrasounds and blood work, as often as four to five times a week during each 28-day cycle. Tony and I were excited about trying a new approach. The doctor encouraged Tony to get involved in this process by learning to give me the injections. He began to practice, and soon was a pro. It was much more convenient for him to give me the injections at home than to go to an office, especially on weekends.

One month went by with no conception, and then another. I felt I was spending all my time visiting the doctor and taking medications. We even planned vacations and our social life around these frequent appointments.

Four uneventful months later, the doctor decided to do an exploratory laparoscopy. During this surgery, he used a scope to look for internal problems such as endometriosis and blockage of the fallopian tubes. Thankfully, he found no significant problems. On the other hand, I was also frustrated with the fact that I still was unable to conceive if there were no other problems.

The doctor decided to use a higher dose of medication, and the very next month I became pregnant. Since I was monitored so closely, the pregnancy was detected unusually early. I was thrilled! Yet somehow I did not feel truly peaceful about it. I went back for a second pregnancy test a week later. That afternoon I received a phone call. When I heard the voice of my doctor, instead of the nurse, I knew he did not have good news. My pregnancy hormone level was not increasing as it should. I remember his words so dearly. "I'm sorry, but it looks like you are going to miscarry." The lump in my throat prevented words; only tears would come. Tony and I began to pray for this tiny little life. We prayed that perhaps the test had been wrong. But in a few days, the bleeding started and we lost our second child. Once again disappointment and grief filled my heart. Praying with faith became harder and harder. I wanted an immediate solution from God. I was growing weary of walking ever so slowly through this valley. It seemed that everywhere I looked, there were pregnant women. I found it increasingly difficult to hear of friends who were pregnant. Yes, I was happy for them, but I wanted a child too. It also became more difficult to attend baby showers, seeing all of the soft, cuddly baby things. It only made my heart ache more for a child. I began to avoid going to them. Then I would feel guilty about having these feelings and would try to hide them. In some ways, I felt my life was becoming a charade.

At this time in my life, God began softening my heart and opening my ears to His voice about the valley in which I walked. He brought to mind the story of Shadrach, Meshach, and Abednego in Daniel 3. King Nebuchadnezzar had them cast into the fiery furnace since they would not bow down and worship him. They knew God was able to deliver them from the furnace, but even if He did not, they knew He was still 'The Most High God.' Verse 25 says **".. Look! I see four men loosed and walking around in the midst of the fire without harm and the appearance of the fourth is like a son of the gods!"** I knew at that moment that my God was walking with me in the midst of my fiery furnace. He did not prevent me from going into this deep valley, but He was certainly there with me all the way. There was much I wanted Him to do that He did not do. But in the midst of my valleys, His gentle and loving arms lifted and carried me. I knew that I must submit to God's perfect will for my life and not my own. My personal desires and requests might not be God's plan at all. That was hard to accept, but little by little, He began to change me. I began to see that the most important thing in my life was that God loved me and nothing occurred outside of His providential will. I realized that I might struggle and hurt, and that I might not find all the answers. I began to have a renewed confidence in my Sovereign God.

The Bible commands Christians to do some difficult things. **"Rejoice in the Lord always"** (Philippians 4:4). **"Rejoice always. In everything give thanks..."** (I Thessalonians 5:16,18). **"Consider it all joy ... when you encounter various trials"** (James 1:2). This seemed quite unreasonable, but slowly I began to learn that I could not know His triumph without first experiencing His testing. I realized that healing from my pain and heartache, would come only through Him. These things neither happened immediately, nor did the pain go away instantly. It was a slow process of continuing to inch down the path in my valley, but I knew I was walking hand-in-hand with the King.

I continued to use the medication and to make frequent visits to the doctor. I was trusting, as best I knew how, that God's will would be done in our lives regarding a child. Then, three months later, I learned again that I was pregnant. Two blood tests showed that my pregnancy hormone levels were increasing normally. The doctor felt that this pregnancy was off to a good start. Morning sickness came immediately and was so severe that I had difficulty working. When I was about four weeks pregnant I began bleeding one day at work. Fear filled my heart, and I raced home. Fortunately, Tony was already there, and drove me to the doctor's office. Anxiety was clearly written on our faces and tears streamed down my cheeks. Imagine our shock to see on the ultrasound screen, not one, but two little flickering lights, indicating the heartbeats of two tiny lives in my womb! The doctor determined that the cause of the bleeding was a clot in my uterus. His primary concern was the danger of the clot sloughing off and pulling with it one or both of the embryos. The best thing that could happen would be for the clot to naturally dissipate. The doctor cautioned us not to become too excited over the two embryos. This happens frequently, he explained, and sometimes only one survives. I was immediately put on bed rest, and my progress was carefully monitored. Tony and I could hardly contain our joy that the Lord might be blessing us with twins. The bed rest gave me plenty of time to pray and seek God. We told a few of our closest friends and they began to pray. As the days went by, the ultrasounds began to show that indeed the clot was breaking up and the babies were growing. At about eight weeks, my specialist released me to go back to my regular obstetrician. I had quite an eventful pregnancy with periods of bed rest off-and-on during the entire time, due to threatened pre-term labor. Many friends prayed along with us for these two precious little lives growing inside of me.

On December 2nd the Lord gave us two wonderful sons, Colin Lloyd and Preston Vance. They arrived only three-and-a-half weeks early and were completely healthy. This was the Lord's perfect plan for our lives. When everything had previously seemed to be right from my perspective, only He knew the perfect timing. As I write now, tears fill my eyes and joy overflows my heart for these two precious gifts from God. How thankful we are for them!

During our four years of infertility and two miscarriages, the Lord drew Tony and me closer as husband and wife. These struggles caused us to lean on each other in a special way for emotional and spiritual support. As a couple, our relationship with the Lord grew much deeper, and God became the first priority in our lives. I came to know Him as my El-Shaddai, my All-Sufficient One. He was my Protector. He upheld me through each painful month of longing for a child. He supported me through each disappointing miscarriage. He sustained me through all my fears and frustrations.

As time goes by, I continue to gain an increased perspective on these struggles. I have learned that God called me to walk through these valleys, and that He provided the grace to guide me through them. He is a good and loving God who knows and feels our pain. Matthew 5:4 says, **"Blessed are those who mourn, for they shall be comforted."** Christians are not exempt from pain and suffering, but we serve the God of all comfort. It is my desire that these experiences serve positively to touch lives. I am thankful that God could use my trials to help and encourage others. The pain is never forgotten, and I would not want to forget how my God carried me through the valleys. I look forward to one day meeting Jehovah-Raah, the Lord my Shepherd, in Heaven with my other two babies in His arms. Praise be to our gracious and bountiful God!

PSALM 23
The Lord is my shepherd, I shall not want.
He makes me lie down in green pastures;
He leads me beside quiet waters. He restores my soul;
He guides me in the paths of righteousness for His name's sake.
Even though I walk through the valley of the shadow of death,
I fear no evil; for Thou art with me; Thy rod and Thy staff, they comfort me.
Thou dost prepare a table before me in the presence of my enemies;
Thou hast anointed my head with oil; My cup overflows.
Surely goodness and lovingkindness will follow me all the days of my life,
And I will dwell in the house of the Lord forever.

MY ROSE AMONG THE THORNS

By Patty Wade

"Infertility", the diagnosis read as I got into my car that hot summer afternoon. "No, I am not infertile," I said aloud as I wiped the tears from my eyes. It was the first time I had seen it written about myself regarding my ongoing pursuit to have a baby. The word pierced my heart as I pondered the previous months that brought me to this point.

My husband and I had been married almost five years when we decided to begin our family. Although I did not conceive for the first few months, we weren't discouraged. Being youth sponsors in a large church, while holding full-time jobs kept us very busy.

Finally after nine months of praying and hoping, my doctor confirmed that I was pregnant! I thanked God for this life and I felt good that I was not one of those "infertile women" like some of my close friends. We decided to keep our little surprise a secret from our friends until I was at least three months along. We shared our news with our families, and they, like us, began planning and looking forward to the day our little one would arrive and change our lives.

Eight weeks later our plans were shattered when I lost my baby to a miscarriage. The days that followed proved to be trying and difficult. Although we never held or saw the baby, we had to mentally bury our dreams for this child.

For several days after the miscarriage I searched the Scriptures for verses of comfort. In my journal I recorded these thoughts: **"I love You, Lord, because You hear my voice and my supplication, because You have inclined Your ear to me. Therefore I shall call upon You as long as I live" (Psalm 116:1-2).** Although I am reluctant to write these words because they are so freshly painful, I want it to be recorded that God is faithful always in good times and in times of need or pain and that God cares for us. Psalm 116 has been such a source of comfort. Verse 5 says, **"Gracious is the Lord and righteous, Yes, our God is compassionate."** I have tasted and seen that the Lord is good. The Holy Spirit has ministered to me through comfort and by bringing Scripture to my memory. Thank You Father for keeping me close to You and for reminding me so quickly to turn to You and Your Word as my source of strength. Help me to remember enough of the pain to minister to those who may go through a similar experience. Help me to accept things like this that I cannot change, especially in front of my unsaved friends who so desperately need to hear about You and Your love..." God's Word truly sustained my spirit during this time.

I was also ministered to by the encouragement from the friends and family around me. So many women called to tell me that they had suffered a miscarriage also, which made me feel less lonely. I received several cards from friends and family. The support made me realize how important it is to minister to those around me, and how important fellow Christians are in my life. With all the good support also came the "thoughtless" remarks. One friend told me that she didn't trust my doctor. Another inferred that because of the procedure I had, I risked the chance of never conceiving again. Along with these remarks came others from people who really didn't know what to say. "It was probably a blessing, something may have been wrong; there will be others" and "at least you weren't too far into your pregnancy" were a few of the remarks. The thought I had to keep before me was that all these people truly did care; some expressed it well and others were at a loss for words.

Time helped dim the pain and after a few months my doctor approved our trying to begin our family again. Five more months came and went quickly. Staying busy in our jobs and ministry helped keep me from staying discouraged. I visited my gynecologist in the spring. She recommended a laparoscopy to see if anything was wrong internally. It was on her bill that I first read my diagnosis: **"INFERTILITY."** Perhaps it was time for me to face up to these words. The dictionary defines infertility as the inability to conceive after one year or the inability to carry a pregnancy to a live birth. Although I knew this didn't have to be a permanent diagnosis, I did realize that I must carefully search to do everything within my means to conceive our baby. I knew also that God had walked with us every day of our marriage, and He had a perfect plan for us, which at this time included infertility and His grace to endure it. Once again God's Word comforted me. A verse I kept before me was Psalm 113:9, **"He settles the barren woman in her home as a happy mother of children"** (NIV).

Months and years of infertility can create extreme pressure on a marriage. During my difficult times, I always had the support of my husband. He comforted me when I thought I was pregnant but found I wasn't. He expressed love and encouragement to me, even though I knew he longed for a child of his own. Our outlook was that God had blessed us so richly with family, friends, and a ministry that we really couldn't stay depressed about our childless status. In His time, we would have a child.

I went ahead with my laparoscopy in the fall. The surgery, a small incision near the belly button, allows the doctor to look at the female organs for any problems. The prognosis was good. Some endometriosis was spotted but not enough to prevent me from conceiving. A hysterosalpinagogram (dye inserted into the tubes) showed there were no obstructions. Since the tests revealed no specific problems, reluctantly I changed doctors and began seeing an infertility specialist. My regular gynecologist had been so supportive, but we both agreed this was a needed step.

Entering this territory was a whole new world for me – a world I didn't particularly enjoy. It took me on a roller coaster of monthly highs and lows. Because infertility is so elusive, I strongly encourage everyone who has problems conceiving to go to a specialist. I learned of women who had the simplest things wrong that a specialist could easily detect and resolve. However, sometimes it is a difficult process. It's amazing how many types of procedures are used to eliminate possible causes of infertility!

For the next year, I felt like a guinea pig while the doctor, my husband, and I tried many different tests and procedures. A small problem was a low level of progesterone during the latter portion of my cycle. Corrective medication was prescribed and for months following, it was faithfully administered to no avail. I truly feel for anyone who goes through any length of infertility. It is an emotional and physical strain.

One year after my first pregnancy, I recorded these thoughts in my journal:

"Dear God, I can hardly believe that it's been one year since I first realized I was pregnant. I'm so glad we can't see into the future... I praise you Father that you have sustained me. That's not to say I haven't hoped or dreamed about being pregnant. It's all in Your hands – Your perfect timing and will is sufficient."

After two years of dealing with my thorn in the flesh, my doctor and I decided it was time for a second surgery. This time he would perform a laparoscopy and use a laser to burn away any endometriosis. The surgery seemed to go well and my doctor didn't see any reason why I couldn't conceive.

During the next year we tried to do everything possible to conceive a child. I decreased my work schedule and tried to reduce other outside activities. Concerned family and friends shared much advice from taking cough syrup to eating certain foods. When fertility drugs were used, the family shared their fears about "tampering with nature." Though at times we felt that the unspoken words, "childless couple," were seen by some as a dreaded terminal condition, God continually gave us reassuring peace.

We had been waiting nearly four years by this time. On New Year's Day, I recorded some prayer requests for the coming year. At the end of my long list I wrote, "...and if You so will, we will have a child..."

Isaiah 55:8 says: **"For My thoughts are not your thoughts, neither are your ways, My ways, declares the Lord."** It was during this year that we began to seriously look at our alternatives. Adoption seemed to be a reasonable possibility for us to explore. We began requesting information from various agencies. We decided to keep our search private and only share our desire with our families and some close friends.

We prayerfully chose an agency that we felt had the same philosophies and beliefs we did. Filling out the application was truly a chore. Both of us had to write biographies, feelings about our childhood experiences, beliefs and goals. The total process from beginning to end included over 50 pages of various papers and forms. Finally the day came to mail our application.

In my journal I wrote, *"I pray that God will sincerely lead us through this road of adoption, especially in the area of finances. I claim the name of Jehovah-Jireh, (which means) God will provide, financially, emotionally, spiritually, and most importantly provide a child according to His perfect will."*

Five days later I received an unexpected bonus at work. It was an answer to prayer and the beginning of our adoption fund. Jehovah-Jireh, God will provide!

Once we were accepted by the agency, our waiting game began. I must say that adoption is not the answer for everyone. It's a decision that must be made by each couple. Both partners need to feel ready for this step and comfortable with the fact that this child is not biologically theirs. Viewing adoption not as a "second best choice" is important. For us, God had not opened the door of conception but seemed to open another door. We both had quiet assurance and peace as we began the long walk through the adoption process.

Weeks turned into months and months into a year. A little over a year had passed when we decided to have some friends over for dinner. Having a daughter who was adopted, they had been such a source of encouragement during our process. We had tried to have them over for some time, but our schedules never seemed to fit together. That afternoon as I was in the kitchen preparing the meal for our friends, my husband ran in the back door. He said the agency had contacted him at his office with some important news that they would only share if both of us were on the phone. Very quickly we dialed the number with each of us on an extension. When our caseworker came on the phone, she said, "Congratulations, a little boy has been born for you!" We were stunned, excited, thankful, and scared. For the next hour, we talked with her about him, his birth parents and, of course, when we could pick him up.

After we hung up the phone, we cried with thankfulness for this precious life. My husband returned to his office and I continued to prepare dinner for our friends. We anticipated sharing our news with them when the right moment became available. When they arrived that night, we tried to be as normal as possible. As we were preparing to eat, our friends asked, "Have you heard anything from the agency?" We began to grin, looked at each other, and they knew. Because they had adopted one year earlier, they truly understood the feelings that were overwhelming us. We thank God that in His divine providence, these special friends came to dinner that particular night to share in our unexpected joy after nearly a year of trying to get together.

That day began four long weeks of difficult waiting. It was perhaps the most difficult time since we had started trying to have a family five years prior.

Similar to the preparations for having a baby naturally, there was much to do. Our church, friends, and family were so generous to us. Through showers and gifts, everything needed for this little one was given. Financially, money was a concern, but our Heavenly Father provided the amount needed when the time came. During this time of waiting, we were able to share freely how God had provided our precious son. His story is a beautiful tribute to God's faithfulness in his life and ours.

During the last week, I struggled, doubting if we would ever see this child. Psalm 84:11b says, **"No good thing does He withhold from those who walk uprightly."** Would we see this child? Would there be any problems in the approval cycle? My mind constantly replayed these questions. Only God's grace sustained us.

One afternoon the phone rang on my desk at work. I hesitated as I did every time the phone rang during those expectant days. It was my caseworker. "When can you pick up this little boy?" she asked. I could hardly get the words out through my tears, "You wouldn't be kidding me, would you?"

The next morning we went to the agency to meet and bring back our son. Many strange feelings filled our minds as we traveled to our destiny that summer morning. What would he look like? Would we really love him as our own? We would be going as two and coming back as three. How would our lives be impacted?

When we got to the agency, the first hour was spent reviewing papers, fulfilling financial obligations and learning about legal matters. Finally our caseworker asked us, "Would you like to meet your son?"

We got up and went across the hall. As the door was opened, we had our first glimpse of our little angel from heaven. If there was ever love at first sight, this was truly it. We wept as our son was placed in my arms. God's timing was perfect. On the trip back, as I watched our little son sleeping, the Holy Spirit reminded me of James 1:17a, **"Every good and perfect gift is from above..."** (NIV).

My thorn in the flesh, infertility, still sticks me in the side occasionally. But if you look really closely at the thorns, you will see a beautiful rose. This rose has the face of a blue-eyed boy. And without the thorns, there would be no rose. **"Let them know that it is Your hand, that You, O Lord, have done it"** (Psalm 109:27) (NIV).

PART II
STILLBIRTH

"Come to Me, all who are weary and heavy-laden, and I will give you rest. Take My yoke upon you, and learn from Me, for I am gentle and humble in heart; and you shall find rest for your souls." Matthew 11:28-29

WHEN CLICHES ARE NOT ENOUGH

by Sheila Byerly Brooks

"We attempted to produce smiles for those who dared venture onto our path with their pat phrases and overworked cliches."

The spring morning was sunny, yet brisk at our rural home as I sat at the old Singer sewing machine mending the rips and tears of three active children. Amy, our six year old, was by now settled comfortably in her first grade classroom, while three year-old Jeremy and almost two year-old Anna played busily around their very pregnant mother. This morning was typical of most other tranquil country mornings externally, but internally there was an almost unconscious apprehension of events that were soon to follow. As the Singer needle raced along the seams, my mind was swiftly reviewing the events of a busy weekend, searching for the source of this uneasiness that had consumed me only moments ago. Saturday morning had been spent helping my mother-in-law plant her garden, and the afternoon found me cooking for a church picnic which we would attend that evening. And of course, there had been the two worship services to attend on Sunday and the Sunday School class to teach. With almost six months of pregnancy behind me and the basic requirements of three young children and one busy husband, my mind was almost convinced I was just tired and needed a bit of rest.

By the time the mending was finished and put aside, the tears were inevitable. I had unsuccessfully searched for a logical explanation for what I hoped were unsubstantiated fears. There was no mistaking the fact that this baby, whose constant activity brought me much discomfort, was now silent – or perhaps just quieter – or maybe just settling down. After all, wasn't my size proof that this precious one was living in very close quarters and could no longer move as freely?

As I slowly made my way to the kitchen phone, and through my tears searched for the doctor's number, my heart was crying out to God, and yet no words were coming. In the days to follow I would learn experientially what the Apostle Paul meant in Romans 8:26 by "groaning which cannot be uttered." By the tone in the nurse's voice, I knew that our baby was in serious trouble. After a quick call to my astounded husband, Philip and I left the children with his mother and drove the forty-five minutes to the doctor's office, with the exchange of few words.

We were quickly whisked into the cold examination room, where we watched as the nurse attempted to find a heartbeat, and then grew almost hopeless as the doctor made an unsuccessful endeavor to locate that tiny beating muscle. Within minutes I was undergoing a more sophisticated ultrasound at the hospital. Philip was not allowed to be with me, and I was not allowed to see the images projected onto the screen. We both needed to see those lifeless images of our little one, but it was against hospital policy.

We soon heard our doctor calmly explain, with almost a hint of indifference in his voice, that our baby was dead. Briefly, he informed us that labor could be artificially induced, or we could wait for natural labor to occur. Even though this doctor had declared emphatically that his judgment was correct, we knew of cases in which doctors had totally missed the mark. After explaining our pro-life conviction, we left the office with an appointment to return in one week, should labor not begin.

No human words could bring peace or comfort at this point. Philip and I stopped at a nearby restaurant for lunch, but neither of us could eat. Like rushing water about to break forth over a dam, so were our tears. I was able to repress them until we were once again in the car and headed home. It was then that the dam broke, and the tears were therapeutically released, only to be followed by the most-asked question in human history, "Why, Lord?" There was no bitterness or contempt towards God, just a sincere longing to know God's heart and mind at this point.

Some of our questions were good and caused us to earnestly take inventory of our commitment of Jesus Christ. Was God trying to show us something? Would we serve Him no matter what happened? Later, we were capable of seeing our situation in a clearer perspective, knowing that the Creator of the universe, the Redeemer of all those who will trust in His shed blood as the perfect payment for sin, could not and would not give us more than we could bear. 1 Corinthians 10:13 promised us that we could victoriously endure the test. However, some of our questions were influenced by Satan, the arch-enemy of our souls. Scripture refers to him as the *"accuser of the brethren."* Was God punishing us for some unknown sin? Would friends think we were outside of God's will for our lives? After all, Philip had pastored for a number of years, but was now working with his father in a family-owned business. Would others realize that it was God who had closed the door of pastoral ministry for the present time, or would we be accused of failing to follow His leadership? All these questions and more were mulled over in our minds on that difficult drive home.

By the time we had shared our news with Philip's family and picked up our children, we were emotionally drained. Even though we were both Bible college graduates and knew God's Word, Satan in his subtlety had already moved on the scene and subjected us to his cruel and groundless accusations. It was during this stressful time that the Biblical account of Job became so authentic to us. As a college student, I had claimed Job 23:10 as a trustworthy affirmation of God's pledge to take the fearful, painful experiences of life and use them as sandpaper against my own sinful human nature. The exclamation point of the solution to Job's problem came when he realized that God wanted to polish him like gold, rather than leave him in his dull mediocrity. At this point, this truth was comfort enough in our search for a reason.

The agonizing week that followed brought sleeplessness, frustration, anxiety, grief, and more tears. Every move made by the children was a source of irritation to me. I loved them deeply, but I was now consumed with such intense grief, and even a false sense of guilt. What had I done wrong? Had I not eaten properly, or exercised regularly, or rested sufficiently, or had I done too much? I had never let any of my other pregnancies slow me down; yet had my lifting, or reaching, or bending hurt our baby this time? Was there a genetic problem for which I was responsible? Was there a link between this baby and my second pregnancy, which ended in miscarriage? Would God choose to perform a miracle to demonstrate His power and our faith? Could the doctor have made a mistake? Time would teach me that less searching for immediate answers and more resting in Him produce peace in my inner spirit.

Late in the evenings when Philip would arrive home from work, I would long to pour out my innermost feelings to him, but it was almost as though they were locked inside. I knew he was hurting too, but I was already learning that few people, including my family and friends, wanted to share my burden. There was almost the fear that he would become uneasy, like many of them, and avoid my company. Such an emotion had no justification in my husband's actions; nevertheless, in my mind, the emotion was very real. Words were not as plentiful as the teardrops, so during those lonely nights we would just lie in bed, hold each other, and pray until my weary mate would fall asleep from physical and mental exhaustion. It was then that I would weep until it seemed as though every drop of moisture in my body was drained. For hours I would lie awake, longing to feel the baby kick and almost convincing myself that there had been a slight movement.

Even though few words brought lasting comfort, hearing the breaking voice of my mother over the telephone, after learning the sad news from me, was medicinal. Isaiah 66:13 compares God's comfort to that of a mother. She offered no cliches and no possible explanations. She just cried with me and shared the pain that she had experienced in an early miscarriage. I had never known that she had grieved in much the same way as I was presently grieving, yet because of the Holy Spirit's residence in our lives, I could once again feel His restoring power in my life, just as she had also come to experience.

The week ended in much the same way as it had begun. Each new day began with a cry for God's help and strength. This day would be no different – only more intense. Today was Sunday, May 8, Mother's Day. The hymns were sung, the prayers were prayed, and the message was preached. All my energy was expended in merely getting through the day. It must have hurt Philip deeply, too. Because of the significance of the day, the children were beginning to enter into our pain in more depth. We deliberately kept the channels open for our children to ask questions and know the entire truth. Regardless of their young age, we wanted them to face reality and at the same time begin to understand God's comfort for us and His care for our baby. We encouraged them to cry and talk to us, and as a result, the Lord used their sweet, child-like faith and trust to minister to our aching hearts.

Our pastor had visited the previous week and left the quote of one of his mentors with us. We tenaciously clung to those words in the days to follow: "God is too good to do evil and too wise to make a mistake." Because of this fundamental truth, we were able to keep our perspective of God clear and unobscured. Over two weeks had passed since we learned of our baby's death. Physically, I was beginning to feel ill, and emotionally, I was not ready to be separated from my baby. Because of the gradual loss of amniotic fluid, I barely looked pregnant. Sitting side-by-side in the doctor's office, Philip and I were instructed to arrive at the hospital by six o'clock the following morning. Unlike most cases, I had not gone into labor naturally, and now to avoid infection, induced labor was a must. As though hanging onto one last strand of hope, we asked for one additional scan. Belligerently the doctor retorted, "This baby is dead. You don't need another scan." After quietly reassuring him that we would pay for the service, he cooperated, and this time we were allowed to see the screen.

Sufficiently convinced, we made arrangements for my parents to come from their home about two hours away and stay with our children. I saw the pain in my mother's eyes as she hugged me good-bye. The hour-long drive to the hospital was spent clasping hands and enduring the quietness of the early morning. Within a few hours it would all be over, and we would be back home once more.

Immediately upon my arrival on the delivery floor, a nurse with little compassion prepped me. Sensing her wrong judgment of me, I explained that my intentions were not to abort a live baby, but that my baby was dead. As I talked, my voice trembled, which prompted her to usher my husband to my side. Within ten minutes pitocin began to drip into my veins, and almost spontaneously the contractions followed. Philip hovered over me, stroking my brow and telling me how much he loved me.

The attending OB doctor had informed us that labor would be short due to the small size of the baby. Fifteen minutes passed, and with each passing minute the contractions became strong enough to accomplish delivery. Noon came and went, and the contractions persisted. Monitors proved that, medically speaking, our baby should have already been delivered. Unable to see any progress, the doctor increased the pitocin again and added prostaglandin to my agony. Violent contractions began with virtually no recovery time in between. Still, there was little dilation. This scene would repeat itself many times before relief would come. Since I was making no progress, I was sent to a private room to eat and rest for the remainder of the night.

Early on Sunday morning, the grueling routine began again. The prostaglandin brought unexpected side effects - nausea and vomiting, diarrhea, and loss of control from the waist down. The pain was almost unbearable, nothing like my previous labors. My hips were like lead, and no matter how desperately I tried to lift my body from the bed, I could not. Several times medication was injected to alleviate the pain, but was soon discontinued because it stopped the contractions. The doctor continued the use of prostaglandin on into the Sunday night hours. Finally, a mild sedative was prescribed to provide little catnaps in an effort to combat my absolute exhaustion.

As morning approached, Philip did his best to be reassuring and comforting, but hope was evading me. There was no doubt that he had been struggling with me. The lines on his face witnessed his own suffering and weariness. Somehow I mustered what seemed to be my last ebb of strength to clearly instruct him, "No more prostaglandin!" I could feel myself drifting in and out of reality, and I seriously wondered if this was death. I could hear my doctor talking quietly to Philip just outside the door, and I could hear Philip tell him my instructions. He quickly returned to my side to let me know that it was almost over. My blood pressure was dropping significantly and a Caesarean section had been ordered.

A nurse quickly prepped me for surgery, and as she performed her duties she shared her faith in Christ with me. As she rolled my stretcher out into the hallway, the assisting physician stepped forward to tell me that he would be praying during the procedure. How good the Lord is! Not only had He promised to be with me, but also He had sent two chosen believers to care for me.

I chose to remain awake. This would be the only opportunity to see our baby together. As the nurse lovingly placed our tiny, blanketed daughter in my arms, we were forced to say both our hello and good-bye in but a few brief moments. Her tiny fingers and toes were all in place, her eyelashes and brows not yet present, but to us she was like a beautiful little china doll – so delicate, so sweet, and so loved. As she was taken from our arms, we both began the gradual process of letting go and entrusting her into the hands of her Heavenly Father. Even as David said in the Psalms that he would someday go to his beloved son, we would someday share in our daughter's joy forevermore.

Arrangements had been made prior to my hospital entrance to bury Abigail Faith in a cemetery relatively near our home. As I sat alone in my hospital room on that bitter cold Tuesday morning, I wondered what our pastor was sharing with our family and a few friends at the small graveside service. In my mind I could visualize that tiny white coffin covered with miniature pink roses and white baby's breath. How I needed to be there; yet physically, it was impossible. Later I would learn that it could have been an important step in the process of letting go. While in surgery, we had been given a picture of Abigail, so my morning was spent alone with her image. Had it not been for the presence and comfort of Christ in my life during those hours, the loneliness would have been overwhelming.

The afternoon brought my mother-in-law and two sisters-in-law with snapshots of the funeral. After getting the children settled with my mother and father and saying good-bye to my sister, sisters-in-law, and brothers, Philip came with the taped message of the service. This was so very difficult, but God's grace was already proving sufficient.

As the weekend neared I begged to be released. I could not miss Anna's second birthday on Friday. What a special homecoming it was! Philip's mother had prepared a splendid meal with birthday cake included, and my mother had dressed the children just so to meet my approval. Never again would it be convenient to take Amy, Jeremy, or Anna for granted. It felt so good to be a family again.

In the weeks and months to come, we learned significant first-hand lessons in ministering to hurting people. We attempted to produce smiles for those who dared venture onto our path with their pat phrases and overworked cliches. "Just put it behind you... at least you have three other healthy children... she's better off... she would probably have been retarded"... and on and on they went. They were all well-meaning friends and family who had never learned just to **"... weep with them that weep" (Romans 12:15)**. Empty words were not appropriate. I needed a friend to walk alongside me and share my burden. The Lord did not fail me; once again He proved His faithfulness by sending such a friend. I had only known her casually from church, but a bond developed between us that time has nurtured and strengthened. She shared no advice, but she listened when I needed to voice my innermost feelings. She never shunned the subject of Abigail's death as most had done, but rather encouraged the conversation in an atmosphere of comfort and ease.

Eight years have passed since our little one went Home. As a family, we stood over her graveside on what would have been her eighth birthday this year. The tears and pain, somewhat dulled by time, were still there for all of us, but the peace and consolation from our Heavenly Father has intensified and matured us during these past years.

We have learned experientially what no formal training could have taught us in dealing with hurting people. Perhaps this is the ministry God has been preparing for us. We now have an inside, up-close view of pain and the impact that we can have in the lives of those who endure such anguish.

Though the testing was severe, through it I also came to better know the husband God has so graciously given to me. The Lord used the lens of adversity to magnify the strength and gentleness that this man had possessed all along. During many arduous days, he allowed me to express my moodiness and loved me in spite of it. On the day of Abigail's delivery, the Lord had ministered to his heart through the words of Psalm 16:11, and now my husband was tenderly leading me into a more complete understanding of this truth.

"Thou wilt show me the path of life: in thy presence is fullness of joy; at thy right hand there are pleasures forevermore" (KJV).

Yes, there are still those times when the question of "why" emerges. And when we sit at the feet of Jesus one day, His purpose and plan will be totally unveiled to us. Until then we rest in Him who knows the beginning from the end. He has proven Himself so very faithful!

That Familiar Sound

By Philip Brooks

Y ou have heard it over and over again. You know the piercing ring as the hammer strikes the chisel. God, the great sculptor, is hard at work again. That piercing ring and the torturous pain make the best of us want to run and hide. Even though we believe we are strong, we men are often afraid of the pain that penetrates far deeper than our flesh and forces its way into our very heart and soul.

Since becoming a Christian, I have experienced God's continuous work in my life, gently forming me into a serviceable tool for Him. Over the years I certainly had pressures that were comparable to muted blows on the chisel, which chipped away small fragments. One sunny spring day in May, it suddenly felt like God was using His largest hammer. The most powerful blow that I ever endured came with a phone call from my very distraught wife with the news that our unborn child was probably in distress. Truthfully, I was almost speechless. What do you say to the one you love so much when you are afraid that you might say the wrong thing?

What am I going to do? What will I say? What if our baby really is dead? These and many other questions raced through my head as I sped home from the office. When I walked into our home, all I could do was hold her in my arms and let her sob. As we drove to the doctor's office, I tried to reassure her of God's love for all of us, and that He was still in control. Of course, I also needed to remind myself of those facts, because my pain was severely increasing.

When the doctor's dreaded words were heard, a distinct feeling overtook my soul. It was simultaneously one of disbelief and overwhelming faith. I refused to believe our baby might be dead, and at the same time I was thinking about someone who is stronger and more powerful than this doctor. Next on my mind was Sheila's reaction. I had seen many times that her faith was actually stronger than mine, yet I knew her emotions would possibly be completely out of control. "God, you have to perform a miracle, you just have to, please!" I was feeling her pain and she was feeling mine, and we were in agreement that we would not act in haste when the baby might indeed still be alive.

Understanding our options, we left to return home, only to face WHY?! WHY is this happening to us? Oh, I thought all the really spiritual people didn't question God. So, maybe I was not so spiritual. Could that be why the hammer was hitting harder and the chisel cutting deeper? I knew this trial would test the sincerity of my faith. I wanted to help my wife. I needed the Lord to help me to understand her feelings and emotions. I wanted Him to give me the right words to say that would be comforting; this silence was driving me crazy! I longed to take away her pain. A few halting sentences came, but I really doubted if they were helping her. I knew without a doubt that God knew what He was doing. He never makes mistakes. Would this be enough to soothe the pain in the days and weeks ahead?

The following days were arduous and agonizing. We prayed often together, still believing that it was possible for God to work a miracle and allow our baby to kick again. Yet night after night I would hear Sheila sobbing into her pillow, and my heart would ache for her.

After almost two weeks it was evident that our baby was with the Lord. God had not chosen to perform a miracle. The concern now was the possibility of infection within Sheila's body, so we asked that labor be induced. Shortly after our arrival at the hospital, drugs were administered to induce labor, and we began a lengthy nightmare. Sheila's pain was intense, but our baby would not deliver. It must have been terrible for her; experiencing such pain to deliver a baby that she would never get to cuddle and love and watch grow-up.

After fifty-plus hours of agony, our stillborn baby had to be delivered by caesarean section. I stayed by my wife through it all, because I knew it was so important for her to know that I loved her. Together we touched and held our tiny daughter, Abigail Faith. We counted her fingers and toes and observed that she was fully formed, although she was not full term. Our thoughts were identical, as we later discussed the irrational reasoning of those who purposely abort a living child.

God had not chosen to give our child life outside of the womb, so now I knew that I must be strong for both of us. I needed some "nugget" from God to assure me that this was not a mistake. I went to God's Word while Sheila was in recovery. The date was May 16, so I read the sixteenth Psalm. As I read it, I wept and prayed and didn't seem to be getting much from it, until I read the final verse. There it was — just like a lightning bolt from Heaven – **"Thou wilt shew me the path of life: in thy presence is fullness of joy; at thy right hand there are pleasures forevermore" (Psalm 16:11 KJV).**

How could I even think of wanting to bring her back? She would never have to know the ravages and painful effects of sin in this life. All she would ever know would be joy and pleasure in the presence of an all-loving God.

It was not easy as the days and weeks and months passed. We heard all the old, worn-out cliches and realized that if we were going to seek a ministry out of this situation, we must not be guilty of the same things. I learned that Sheila wanted to talk about our daughter, and even the events of this trial. Most well meaning people were afraid to even mention anything closely connected to the circumstances. All Sheila wanted was someone who was not afraid to talk about the baby's death. She needed to talk about it and to even visit the cemetery often. I learned to listen and learned to love her in an ever-greater way.

The ring of the hammer and chisel are still heard regularly, but we know it is of necessity. We are maybe now a little closer to being the finished product He wants. God's Word had assured us that He will never leave nor forsake us. **To God Be The Glory!**

GOD'S GRACE IS SUFFICIENT

By Sandy Day

Through His Word, God has shown me that He has a purpose and meaning for my life even though I made a mess of things by going my own way and doing my own thing. In Jeremiah 29:11-18 God explains His intention for Israel and for those who are His children. **"'For I know the plans I have for you'" declares the Lord, "'plans for welfare and not for calamity, to give you a future and a hope. Then you will call upon Me and come and pray to Me, and I will listen to you. And you will seek Me and find Me, when you search for Me with all your heart.'"**

From my earliest years, my mom and dad thought I was a rather unusual child. I was high-strung and had a TON of energy! In today's world I would have had many labels added to my name. I remember one day when my mom had taken me to 4-year-old pre-school. I didn't like what they were doing that day, so I left! I walked home. Even though the pre-school was less than a mile from our house, my mom was, to say the least, not very happy to see me. In later years my energy was funneled into things that I thought would make me happy.

At age 13, I began to lead a rebellious and promiscuous lifestyle, which included alcohol and drugs. By the grace of God I graduated from high school. Today, I realize God protected me in many circumstances.

After graduation, I began dating a boy who came from a family that considered church a priority. Just to get his parents off my back, I went to church with them. That was where I heard the Gospel for the first time. As I learned about God's love and forgiveness, I knew I had a LOT to be forgiven! Two Sundays later, I responded to God drawing me to Himself. I called on the name of the Lord for my salvation and repented of my sin. God began to transform my life. I now had a desire to know God and His purposes for me. After confessing my sin, I knew I had to break off the relationship with my boyfriend because of our sinful involvement. Four weeks later I discovered I was pregnant.

I saw abortion as my only option. The moment the procedure was over, I knew I had made a terrible mistake; something that would have lifelong consequences. Today, I am still seeing those consequences. Like so many women in the world today, I learned to hide my pain. In a matter of months, I met a Christian man who became my husband. After we were married, we attended church and worked long hours to build a business together.

But I did not realize that all was not well. Two years into my marriage, I received a call at work from my husband. His message was, "I love you, but I have to go." That day he ended his life. It was a tragedy that awakened me to the power of God's Word. God's Word became my "best friend." As I clung to God's promises, they saw me through the next leg of my journey, one perhaps even more difficult than the last.

After a leave of absence, I returned to my spot in the church choir. In my "usual" seat sat a woman I had never met. As we sat next to each other, we quickly became friends, sharing our struggles and prayer requests. What I didn't know was that when I prayed for my friend's son, Craig – as I was often asked to do – I was praying for my second husband.

I was in the choir the Sunday night Craig surrendered his life to Christ. Amazingly, it was only a short time before he was ministering to me. Three years later we were planning a wedding and were married.

Not long after we were married we became involved in a Sunday School class of young couples who loved the Lord. We soon felt the Lord calling us to become leaders in our class.

As would be expected, our young married Sunday School class was quite prolific! It seemed every other month women were either having babies or telling us they were expecting. For me, pregnancy was a long way off; but as I went to baby showers and saw the happiness my friends were experiencing, I thought it would be wonderful for Craig and me to share this joy also.

After about two years of marriage, I began to feel something was missing. I couldn't understand why Craig could not share his feelings with me or cry around me. I knew God was on the throne and that He answers prayer, so I began to pray about it.

During this time, we conceived our first child. We waited three months before we told anyone, including our parents. I was so happy about our little one that it didn't even matter that I was tired and nauseated. I was careful about what I ate. I exercised. I read about motherhood and all the wonderful things that go along with it. After seven months, I began seeing my doctor every two weeks for more frequent examinations.

One of my friends was due the same day I was. We talked back and forth and compared bellies and weight. When we were 34 weeks along, I was excited for her, and that our little ones could grow up together.

The next morning I began spotting. I knew something couldn't be right. I had 6 weeks to go. I called the doctor and was told to call again immediately if the spotting continued. Since it did, I was instructed to come to the office. I had my bags packed by the time my husband made the 45-minute drive home from work.

On the way to the doctor, I told Craig that something seemed wrong. I hadn't felt the baby move all morning. When we arrived, the doctor used the Doppler and the stethoscope and couldn't find a heartbeat, but reassured me that it could be because of the baby's position. We were referred to a woman's clinic to have an ultrasound. As we nervously waited hand-in-hand, for them to call us in, tears and anxiety began building up about what they would find.

As the ultrasound wand moved over my stomach, the doctor said, "The baby looks good, but there is no heartbeat." I suddenly felt very empty and nervous. Craig and I were left in the room by ourselves. Craig prayed, asking the God who made the lame to walk and the blind to see, that if He wanted our baby to live, He would make his heart start beating again.

I didn't know what to expect. Craig called our parents. Either labor could be induced or we could wait for me to go into natural labor. We chose to go ahead and deliver our child (we had already picked out a girl's name, Caroline Nicole, and a boy's name, James Caleb.)

As we drove to the hospital, we couldn't speak — we simply held hands. When we arrived, we were sent immediately to the maternity floor. It was 5:30 p.m. The nurse told me to change clothes and I would be seen soon. About 6:15, the doctor came in and gave me a suppository called prostaglandin. It had to be inserted and placed on top of my uterus - a painful procedure! Within 30 minutes, I was in heavy labor. The prostaglandin gave me the shakes so badly I couldn't even put my teeth together!

I had an epidural for pain, and 3 pushes later, I delivered our precious son, James Caleb. He weighed 3 pounds 9 ounces and was 19 inches long. What a beautiful baby with big eyes, long eyelashes, and a dimple on his chin. We could see his features matched both of ours. The nurses were kind enough to take pictures of him. The doctor said that because the umbilical cord was so long it had wrapped around his legs and apparently cut off his circulation.

As I held our baby, we looked at our precious little gift from God and remembered that a short life does not mean an incomplete life. We knew that all of this was happening for a reason and that God would use it for His glory.

The next morning flowers came, people called and dropped by, and I described our beautiful Caleb – so tiny, so perfect. After lunch, Craig called the cemetery and the funeral home and went to select a casket for our baby. Late that afternoon when he returned, the visitors had gone. Craig sat on the hospital bed and began to cry out loud. He told me how painful this was for him. As we held each other, I thought about the prayers I had prayed for Craig to be able to share his feelings. I thanked the Lord for answering my prayer in the midst of a very difficult time.

Two days later, I came home with empty arms. Our car was filled with fragrant flowers, but there was no baby to bring to our completed nursery. How devastating!

The burial service was on Friday afternoon. Nearly our whole Sunday School class came. There must have been a hundred friends and family members who came to share our sorrow on that cold, rainy day. As two of our pastors spoke, we sat there holding each other. We could hardly believe what we were facing – a casket with our precious baby in it.

I had so much company at first that reality didn't set in for several weeks. A friend in our church had lost twins. She helped me greatly with the grief and sorrow. We cried together and shared how we felt about statements people had made like, "There was probably something wrong with him," or "You'll have another baby." The bottom line was, I didn't want another baby. I wanted Caleb.

Craig and I found it comforting to lie on the floor in the nursery and listen to Christian music. He seemed to accept our loss as part of God's will for us. I found it harder to accept. I wondered, "Why me? I've been through enough heartache and sorrow."

That year five other women in our church lost eight babies. Seven of our babies are right together at the same cemetery. It is called Babyland, a place we have all grown to treasure.

During that same year, there were eleven healthy babies born in our Sunday School class. In the course of the many baby showers I went to (and gave), it became increasingly difficult for me to be around babies and happy, glowing mothers especially since I hadn't been able to conceive again. On an emotional roller coaster, my heart felt as if it was being torn to pieces at times. Craig couldn't understand how I could sometimes cry one day and be happy the next.

In the fall of that year, I was asked to teach a ladies' Bible study at church. I had taught off and on for several years, but I wasn't sure I could handle it now because we were trying to have another baby. However, I prayed about it and felt the Lord leading me to teach.

It had been seven months since Caleb's death and still no conception. I just knew that because we had lost one child, God would soon bless us with another. But that is not how the Lord operates. He works in His timing, not ours.

In my Bible study class we studied the attributes of God. Even as I was teaching this, I became more and more angry because I hadn't conceived. It had only taken three months with the first baby. Why so long now?

I went to a doctor. He said to chart my temperature for three months. When I awoke in the mornings, before doing anything else, I was to take my temperature and record it. When it began to rise, I would be ovulating. Three more months went by with no conception.

In January, I attended a Women's Conference at our church. The speaker talked about how the devil seeks to rob us of what God is doing in our lives, and, she said we have to make a choice. We can either walk in the ways of God or in the ways of Satan. That day going home in the car, I made my choice. I asked God Almighty to use me in whatever way He would.

On February 12, three days before Caleb's first birthday, during my third month of temperature charting, our pastor preached a sermon I'll never forget. He said there were women in our church who couldn't conceive children, and that, physically, there was nothing they could do about it. That Sunday, I knew the Lord was speaking directly to me. The sermon illustration was Elkanah and his wives, Peninnah and Hannah. Peninnah made fun of Hannah because she could not have children. The Lord had shut her womb (I Samuel 1:5). But Hannah sought the Lord and poured out her heart before Him. She prayed, **"I will give him unto the Lord all the days of his life," (I Samuel 1:11) The Lord heard her cry,** and she conceived and had a son. She named him Samuel. When Hannah brought Samuel to the temple, this is what she said to Eli, the Priest: "Oh, my lord! As your soul lives, my Lord, I am the woman who stood here beside you, praying to the Lord. For this boy I prayed, and the Lord has given me my petition which I asked of Him. So I have also dedicated him to the Lord; as long as he lives he is dedicated to the Lord" (I Samuel 1:26-28).

That Sunday as I sat in the choir, I knew I could not take my bitter, angry feelings home with me. I had to leave them right there at the feet of Jesus. I told the Lord that day that if Caleb was the only child I would have, that was okay. If I never had another child, I would accept that God was enough for me and this was His plan. That day I left church a different person. I no longer carried the load, Christ did.

During all those months of anger, resentment, and bitterness, I had a Shepherd who loved me to the end. He showed me his unconditional love when I was so unlovely to Him. I hurt today for all the women out there who are still bitter toward the Lord. My heart aches for them because I was like that for almost a year, but my Savior reached down and comforted His sheep and restored me.

Sixteen days later I went to the doctor and learned that we had conceived another child. When I got home I dedicated our little one to the Lord. I was excited, but I was also very scared that we could lose another child. At eight weeks we had our first ultrasound. We could see that tiny little heart beating away. I had ultrasounds frequently to make sure everything was going well.

Shopping at the mall one day, I felt something was wrong. I was having a lot of Braxton Hicks contractions. I called the doctor and was told to come by the office. I was 23 weeks along. The doctor said I was 2 centimeters dilated, and 50 percent effaced, and that I should go home and stay in bed. He put me on 5mg of Brethine and a home monitor. When I couldn't sleep, he changed the medication to 2.5 mg every 4 hours. At my appointment the next week he said, "I'm sorry, but you'll need to stay in bed and come here once a week to be checked." I was not happy about this, but I did what he said.

Our Sunday School class was so good to us! They brought meals during the week, and our families alternated weekends. Several girls came and cleaned the house. God's people truly pull together in time of need. Our gratefulness could never be expressed in words.

I didn't realize that the next three months would be a continuous battle to keep our baby in my womb. Every 10-14 days I would go into labor again as the baby had a growth spurt. My medication was increased many times.

When I found out that our baby was another little boy, I began to talk to him and tell him not to be so anxious; that I had waited patiently for him and now he needed to get to 36 weeks. The doctor promised that at 36 weeks I could go off medication and the home monitor.

Staying on bed rest was really good for me. I thought a lot about the Lord, about how wonderful He truly is, and how He sustained me through some very difficult circumstances in my life. Several women had brought me books, which included Bible studies. It was so ironic, but they ALL were about who God is. I have to say that up until this point I thought God was "out to get me – that He was on my tail." I am sure you would understand with as much as I had been through – and ALL of it had happened before I was even 30 years old! I did read all the books and finished ALL the Bible studies. I learned so much about the Lord. I learned that He was good, merciful, gentle, longsuffering, patient, forgiving and that He loved me with an EVERLASTING love (Jeremiah 31:3). Whew! It was just so awesome – I will never forget my "appointed time" on bed rest. God taught me SO much – I have never forgotten His steadfast love and care for me – spiritual care!

During the last two weeks before going off medication, the doctor allowed me to go one place a day. I had to squeeze in a lot of errands before our baby was born! I went off my medication and the monitor at 36 weeks. The doctor assured me that not all moms went into labor after going off medication. I told him in 2 days I would have our little boy.

The next night I was up about every hour, and in the morning during my shower the contractions started. I called the doctor who said, "Come now." When we got to the doctor's office I was going through transition labor. I was 7-10 centimeters dilated and 100 percent effaced. I begged them to let me have the baby there, but I was carried to our car and Craig drove me across the street to the hospital. Thirty-five minutes later I delivered our precious son, Corey Madison. Weighing 6 pounds and 7 ounces, and 20 inches long, he was a darling baby.

All the prayers (even the smallest) I prayed while I was on bed rest were answered. The Good Shepherd takes care of His flock.

Several days passed, and even as we rejoiced over Corey, we remembered our little Caleb and grieved. We never heard him cry or saw him open his eyes or move his hands and feet. But our little boys have taught us so much! Through the loss of Caleb we learned the sufficiency of God's grace. We felt His presence, and His comfort. We clung to His strength in our weakness. God is teaching us His patience as Corey keeps us on our knees in prayer. Oh, that we would be as patient with our children as God is with His children!

When he was three-months-old, we had Corey dedicated at our church. What an emotional time for us and for our church family who had seen God's faithfulness carry us through! I thought again of the story of Hannah and how she dedicated Samuel to the Lord. I had already done that privately, but we wanted to make it official.

When Corey was about ten months old, God gave me a desire to begin a ministry to help other women who had endured losses. As Craig and I began to pray, we saw God put the ministry into place. People would call our home seeking help. Women's groups asked me to come speak and tell the story of what God had done in our lives. God allowed us to comfort others with the comfort we had received from Him. We named our ministry in honor of our firstborn son – Caleb Ministries.

Over the years, I began to realize that a powerful testimony of God's saving grace and comfort was not enough for a powerful ministry to women. God wanted me to be a

pure vessel so that I could be transparent with the women I sought to help. I began by agreeing to complete a Bible study that addressed issues I had tucked away for years and did not ever want to share with ANYONE! That study changed me forever – I understood the forgiveness of God for the abortion that I had tried to hide for so many years.

Not long after completing that study, nine women called the ministry within a three-month period seeking help. Each woman had experienced a stillbirth and each one had an abortion in her past. Craig encouraged me to step out and share what God had done in my life to forgive my sin of abortion. As a result I have been so blessed by the opportunity to share God's answer for the silent pain women still live in due to their own abortion(s). (If you have had an abortion I encourage you to get a copy of my book and Bible study guide for post-abortive women called *"Living in His Forgiveness."*)

Today, Caleb Ministries continues to grow. Letters expressing the pain in the hearts of women arrive in a continual stream. The blessing of ministering to others is one of the rewards of serving Christ. However, my biggest blessing still comes from being a wife and mother. I thank the Lord for my godly husband. The Lord has used him in my life in so many ways; I would not have shared about my abortion without his encouragement. Our son Corey also has a heart to serve God and he brings us so much joy!

As I watch him grow and develop, I am often reminded of Caleb... I wonder if he would like balls and books as much as Corey, or if he would look as much like Craig as Corey does. Those things I will never know, but that's okay, because the Lord has given me His peace. I am grateful that Jesus loved me enough to entrust me with suffering and use it to strengthen my faith and my walk with Him.

God also has a plan for you and has provided for your every need. He offers forgiveness to your soul and comfort for your heart. There is hope for the future. It is my prayer that God's Word will penetrate your heart and you will come to know His love and mercy. I rejoice with you in what God has in store for your life and the transformation He wants to shower upon you.

To my little boys I say,

"Corey, you are a special gift from God… you are a masterpiece.

Caleb, you lived a full life… I'll hold you in heaven."

Love,

Mom

A Brief Life

by Craig Day

A Tribute To James Caleb Day – February 15,1988

"A brief life is not an insignificant life." These are words that Sandy and I received through all the cards and letters that came to our home after the stillbirth of our firstborn son, James Caleb Day. They are words that have deep meaning.

A brief life can still be significant. How so? When your child never gets a chance to have his first breath here on earth, but takes his first in heaven, how could his life be significant? It's all answered in how you measure significance. Is it in the amount of time you spend here on earth or how you live your life? I think it's the latter.

The pain in the loss of a child is so deep you wonder about the meaning of life. Are we here to just "eat, drink and be merry?" Or are we here for a specific purpose? (Jeremiah 1:5) God created all of us for the specific purpose of glorifying Him through our lives. Caleb lived eight months in Sandy's womb. That was his life. He was perfectly formed and created. Yet, God saw it fit to take him directly to heaven, sparing him the curse of this fallen world. Does that mean he lived less of a life? NO! His life was full and complete, just as God had planned it from the beginning: **For Thou didst form my inward parts; Thou didst weave me in my mother's womb. I will give thanks to Thee, for I am fearfully and wonderfully made; Wonderful are Thy works, And my soul knows it very well. My frame was not hidden from Thee, When I was made in secret, [And] skillfully wrought in the depths of the earth. Thine eyes have seen my unformed substance; And in Thy book they were all written, The days that were ordained [for me], When as yet there was not one of them. How precious also are Thy thoughts to me, O God! How vast is the sum of them! If I should count them, they would outnumber the sand. When I awake, I am still with Thee (Psalm 139:13-18).**

Our hearts grieved the earthly loss of our son, fully trusting God as sovereign. Apart from knowing He has a plan for our lives, we have no hope. Life would be meaningless and void of purpose. **"Now faith is the assurance of [things] hoped for, the conviction of things not seen" (Hebrews 11:1).** Faith is believing what you can't see, and trusting that the hand of God is moving in your life for your good and His glory. It took faith for Sandy and me to seek God's purpose in Caleb's death.

The pain does not fully go away with a loss, but God's healing purposes are revealed as time passes. Sandy and I could never have imagined what God would do in our lives and in the lives of countless others through the death of our son; but we could be confident that God was working it out perfectly. Paul wrote in Romans 8:28 about God's perfect work: **"And we know that God causes all things to work together for good to those who** love God, to those who are called according to [His] purpose."

As painful as it is, we have to believe this the way Job felt in all of his adversity. Job responded to his wife's plea for him to, "curse God and die!" by proclaiming, "Shall we indeed accept good from God and not accept adversity?"

God identified with us through His Son Jesus Christ who bore all of the sins of humanity. He knows all of the emotions of loss that you and I have experienced. In His providence, God saw His only Son die on the cross, the most painful of deaths. He knows our pain, yet there is reassuring hope — resurrection day. We are assured of this in the words, **"For the Lord Himself will descend from heaven with a shout, with the voice of [the] archangel, and with the trumpet of God; and the dead in Christ shall rise first. Then we who are alive and remain shall be caught up together with them in the clouds to meet the Lord in the air, and thus we shall always be with the Lord. Therefore comfort one another with these words"** (1 Thessalonians 4:16-18).

We shall see, and be with Him forever, and all those whom you and I loved, who trusted in Him and have joined Him before us.

You see, life is significant if we live it in the light of God's truths. Even a brief life is not an insignificant life. Caleb's life had a purpose.

I love you, Caleb!

Daddy

FAITHFULLNESS THROUGH THE VALLEY

By Karen Shue

After sharing three years together as husband and wife, Ron and I decided it was time for our family to grow. Late one evening after some friends left, I mentioned some changes in my body to Ron. He suggested I take a pregnancy test. Since I just happened to have one on hand, I immediately took his advice. It was positive! We were hesitant about getting too excited because we didn't know if a store-bought test was really accurate. At midnight we headed to the hospital for a blood test. The result confirmed that we were going to be new parents. We were ecstatic! In our excitement we called friends right away to tell them the news. Somehow, I don't think it was quite as exciting to them at one o'clock in the morning.

As the months went by and I felt this precious gift growing inside me, I found myself falling in love with each gentle kick and movement. The nursery was beginning to come together. Showers were being planned, and grandparents were anxiously waiting to get their hands on this new little bundle.

One Friday during my seventh month, Ron took me in for a check-up. When my doctor began doing an ultrasound, he seemed puzzled by what he saw. Trying not to alarm me unnecessarily, he said he was unable to see everything he needed to see. He suggested that I go to another doctor with better equipment. After we left the doctor's office I cried a little. Then I decided not to spend the weekend worrying, since I knew God was in control.

On Monday, Ron and my mother went with me to the hospital. We laughed and joked with the nurses about wanting to know the sex, but as they scanned our baby, the countenance on their faces changed. They became serious, realizing that something was definitely wrong. When the doctor came in and began looking, it didn't take him long to assess what the future held for us. He observed abnormalities in the way the brain was developing. He told us he could not give us any hope because **medically** there was no possibility of the baby surviving. While he was talking to us I thought, "**Medically** our baby may not have a chance, but you don't know what our God can do. We serve a faithful God and His Word says nothing is impossible with Him."

When Ron and I got home we prayed together about our situation. We prayed first for God to heal our baby, knowing that He was able. Even more we prayed for His perfect will to be done in our lives. We were willing to accept whatever that might be. We realized that our only hope was to trust the Lord. We **had** to believe His Word and put our faith in Him. Otherwise, we would have had no hope at all.

I don't mean to imply that we were towers of strength, because we were not, not by any means. We cried, and we hurt deeply, but the Lord did give us an inner strength and peace about our situation. In our humanness, we could not go through this pain and trauma, but God had chosen and entrusted us with this suffering so that we could somehow be used to glorify him.

As family and friends heard the news, the Lord began using our baby to change people's lives. Opportunities opened up for us to speak the name of Jesus and tell of His faithfulness to those whom we might not otherwise have been able to reach. Ron was able to share with many customers about the Lord. One of them became outraged at God and even cursed His name when Ron told him what was happening in our lives. He was suffering from a crippling disease himself and could not understand how God, if He did exist, could let something like this happen! Ron explained to him that God is God. We don't always understand His will for us, but our understanding does not change His sovereignty. We must trust Him wherever we find ourselves.

Another friend, deeply involved with drugs, had just had a healthy baby. She could not understand why something bad like this would happen to such "good" people.

Our God-given strength was not always supernatural. It often took the form of friends and relatives who stood by us through it all. Several of our church friends got together on Saturday mornings to pray for us. I'm sure it pleases God when His people gather together in His name to pray for a special need. It says to Him that we trust Him and believe that He is able to do **"exceedingly abundantly above all that we think"** (Ephesians 3:20). He is right there and all we have to do is call on Him.

A few weeks later we went back to the doctor for another ultrasound. We just knew that when the doctor looked at our baby again the baby would be normal. After all the prayers that went up for this child and the peace the Lord had given us, we were sure that God had healed our baby and the doctors would be totally amazed. Instead we got more bad news. He found a heart defect and some other abnormalities. An amniocentesis revealed a chromosome imbalance called Trisomy 13. Again we were heartbroken, faced with the reality that it might not be God's will for our baby to live. The thought of not holding a baby in our arms, or hearing it cry, or knowing the joy of watching it grow up seemed unbearable. As much as we wanted God's will to be done, we also wanted our baby. To think of not having one hurt more than anyone can imagine. While Ron and I were holding each other and crying, it dawned on us that this may be how our Heavenly Father hurts when His children are separated from Him by sin. He suffers the same hurt for each of us when we reject Him and turn our backs on Him.

Six weeks after we learned of our baby's problems, I went into labor. When we got to the hospital the doctor did an ultrasound, but was unable to find a heartbeat. I still believed that the Lord was going to come through for us and our baby would be fine. That afternoon Ashley Lynn was born. Despite all the doctors and nurses in the room, there was total silence. I kept waiting to hear our baby cry, but she never did. Without a word spoken, Ron and I just held each other and cried. We felt empty, as if our hearts had been torn out. One of the nurses asked if we would like to hold our baby. I reluctantly agreed, but my emotions were in such turmoil I only held her for a few moments and then anxiously gave her back.

Family and friends began coming by to offer comfort. It was hard to receive them because I'd always tried to be so strong. I didn't want them seeing me at the weakest moment in my life! Yet they loved us and cared for us so much that they wanted to be there to share our burden. They were hurting with us. A couple of friends even sneaked a puppy into the hospital. They had searched all day to find just the right one. When I saw the puppy with the pink bow in its hair I thought, "There is no way a dog is going to replace my baby." I later realized I needed that little puppy to nurture and care for since I did not have a baby to hold and love.

Later that evening after things had calmed down, one of the nurses came and very gently began talking with me about my baby. She shared with me the importance of holding her, taking pictures and anything else I felt comfortable doing. Although it sounded strange at first, I began to realize I needed to do it so I could fully accept what had happened. I felt a desire to hold my baby, and I knew I would regret not spending any time with her. They brought Ashley to me all bundled up. As I held her, Ron was right there holding me. We spent a long time with her. When I asked Ron to call the nurse to come get her, he looked at me so brokenhearted and asked if he could hold her. I did not realize that he was hurting and needed to hold Ashley too.

The next morning, as we arrived home, I felt weak and desolate. It didn't seem right to come home with empty arms. I had never felt pain like this agony. I thought I would not make it from one day to the next, but each day the Lord gave me the strength I needed for the day. Some days were worse than others. There were times when my emotions were triggered by slight provocations, which normally would not have affected me. I know I could never have made it through all the hurt and pain without the Lord. He was strong when I was weak.

Even though things did not turn out as we wanted, the Lord was faithful through it all. He has given us the hope of seeing Ashley again one day. As hard as it is to say, I would not change a thing that has happened because I know its purpose is to bring glory to God and touch people's lives for His kingdom.

My story does not end here. Remember, God is faithful! Less than a year after Ashley's death God blessed us with a fine, healthy son. He is the joy of our lives. But we have not forgotten Ashley, and we never will. We thank God for the special gift she has been in our lives.

This is a letter I received from my sister after Ashley's death:

Dear Karen,

I have written this letter in my mind several times, just waiting for the right time to be able to sit down and put it on paper. I have been thinking about you and Ron so often and I pray for you both always. I see Jesus Christ in your life and I have seen Him working and being glorified these past few weeks. I saw Him in your wonderful friends and the love they have for you and each other. I felt so close to Him at the memorial service in the beautiful music and Loran's words, that my tears were out of love for Jesus because I know He loves me and I know He loves you. When all of this first started a few weeks ago, our church circles were starting a Bible study on 1 Peter and the title is "A Faith More Precious Than Gold." That is what has been going through my mind all this time and I have shared with many people that our faith is our most important possession; nothing else really matters in comparison. We don't know what each day will bring, but our faith is what will carry us through. This is what I have seen in your life and it has made a lasting impact on mine. Well, anyway, the night of the memorial service I was supposed to have my circle Bible study. I tried to put it together that Monday morning but I was so depressed I just couldn't do it. We drove to your house, and after spending time with you and seeing your faith in God and feeling the peace that the world cannot understand, I went home and the words flowed from my heart. I decided to tell them about you; to tell them I had witnessed a faith more precious than gold! It was hard to tell and I almost decided against it several times, but God assured me that someone there that night needed to hear it.

I thank God you are my sister in Christ and my sister by birth. I know as the years go by we will grow closer because of His wonderful love. Thank you for all you have let Him teach me. You have blessed my life more than you will ever know.

I love you!
Linda

PART III
EARLY INFANT DEATH

"Trust in the Lord with all
your heart, and do not lean on
your own understanding. In all
your ways acknowledge Him,
And He will make your paths
straight." Proverbs 3:5-6

LOGAN'S GIFT

by Terry Hess

My husband Robert and I have been very blessed in being able to conceive each of the four times we have attempted to have a baby. We didn't have to endure the waiting, the temperature taking, testing, and more waiting that other couples have suffered through. Our first son, Taylor, is now a wonderful young man. Our second baby was miscarried at nine weeks. This story is about our third child.

I remember thinking several times that something was different about this pregnancy, but I couldn't put my finger on it. I mentioned to Robert, that even though I loved this baby, I didn't feel as close to him as I had with Taylor. I thought this was because of my fear of being disappointed again after having miscarried a previous baby. I think now that God was quietly preparing me for what was to come.

In the hours before our second son was born, Robert and I sat in my hospital room pondering the name for our newest child. We finally agreed on a boy's name. That was what we wanted after all! This child would be named Logan.

Labor was to be induced because of my mild case of gestational diabetes. This was fine with me, since I'm not a patient person and was eager to have my child. Taylor had been born naturally and the experience was not pleasant, so I had requested an epidural. I was going to enjoy this birth!

During the middle of the night I was moved into the birthing room for closer observation. (I was told later it was because the nurses had noticed an irregular heartbeat from the baby.) This didn't worry me because both my husband and I had been praying for a healthy baby. As Matthew 7:7 promises, **"Ask and it shall be given to you."**

The events of Logan's birth were beautiful and joyous. Robert was my continual support through the whole process. I actually got to relax and watch Logan being born. He moved through the birth canal rapidly and, as a result, his head wasn't as misshapen as most newborns' tend to be. He emerged at 2:20 p.m. screaming, slippery and wet, with a head full of dark hair. "This one is going to look like us!" was our first thought, since Taylor is blond and we are both brunettes. We were elated! Robert immediately called his parents and mine with our wonderful news.

As I was checking all his fingers and toes, I watched his tiny pink foot slowly turning blue. The nurse swept him from me and started administering oxygen. After getting his footprints and fastening his hospital bracelet, they took him into the nursery for more oxygen, reassuring me that he would be back in a few minutes. I was eager to hold him, but I trusted them to know best. Still weak from the epidural, I couldn't get up and follow, so Robert went with them to the nursery. Able to do little else, I settled back and thanked

God for that beautiful little boy who resembled both Robert and me.

In fifteen minutes, Robert came back and reported they had weighed and measured him and put him in an oxygen tent. Half an hour passed, and I finally asked Robert to see when I could hold him.

Logan's pediatrician had been summoned immediately following his birth. He said Logan needed to be under the respirator an hour or so longer. He encouraged me by saying that when I regained strength, I could go in and see him. In the meantime, my mother arrived, bringing Taylor who had a gift for his new baby brother. He was giving up one of his own little white stuffed bunnies! We shared the Legos that Logan had "gotten" him. He asked where his baby brother was, and we reassured him that he was in the nursery and he could go look at him.

After a quick peek at Logan, Taylor settled down with the Legos and didn't seem concerned that Logan wasn't in the room. However, this was not how I had imagined Taylor meeting his baby brother. I had wanted our whole family to be together that special moment. That moment never came.

A little later the nurses guided me into a wheelchair, and I was off to see my new baby. I was shocked at what I saw. He had monitors attached to his chest and a large acrylic respirator bowl over his head. The pediatrician was looking at x-rays of his heart and lungs. Why did they have all these monitors hooked up to my baby and why did the pediatrician need x-rays? I was confused—was there more to his foot turning blue than they had told me?

Since Robert had spent so much time waiting in the nursery with Logan, and asking many questions, he knew quite a bit about the situation. I would later be most thankful for the information he would receive and relate to me. He reassured me that the monitors were simply tracking Logan's heart rate. The pediatrician also assured us that he could see no problems from the x-rays he had taken. We just needed to wait for him to improve.

Looking up, I saw Taylor peering through the window, and my mother taking pictures. Oh, how grateful I am for all those pictures! As I looked at my new son, I began feeling afraid. This was all very foreign to me. I quickly dismissed the fear. Everything was going to be okay with this baby; God wouldn't let anything happen to an innocent child.

By evening I still had not been able to hold my son. I asked his pediatrician if I would be able to have him in my room overnight. Instead, there was talk about preparing Logan to move to another hospital, better equipped to handle an infant with problems.

All the medical terminology we were hearing was quite confusing to me. Robert suggested that we ask one of our friends, who was an associate of Logan's pediatrician, to explain the situation to us in layman's terms. He arrived shortly, conferred with the doctor, then came and sat on my bed and took my hand. He explained that Watauga County hospital did not have the facilities to determine exactly what was wrong with Logan. He helped us decide which hospital would be best, then with tears in his eyes, prayed with us. In his prayer I can distinctly remember that he asked that God's will be done with our child. Fine, I thought. God could not possibly want anything but good to come out of this situation. Besides, God does not willingly bring affliction or grief to people (Lamentations 3:33).

Robert called one of our best friends, Phillip, to drive with him to the new hospital in Winston-Salem, North Carolina. It was now 1:30 a.m. Saturday morning. I am still amazed how quickly and willingly Phillip came. Thank God for our Christian friends!

The doctor gave me a sedative, and I dozed while they prepared Logan for the trip to Bowman Gray Baptist Hospital, 90 minutes away from Boone, North Carolina. Everyone seemed to be helping out but me, and all I could do was lie there and think. I was convinced now that something was wrong and I wanted to get all the details.

The medics from the emergency van (fog and rain made it impossible to use the helicopter, the preferred transportation) brought Logan to me in an isolette so I could see my baby before they took him away. I was still not allowed to hold him – he was hooked up to all kinds of machines. Logan left in an ambulance with Robert and Phillip following.

The next day was Saturday, and as friends came to visit, the first question they asked was, "Where is he?" I told them briefly what had happened and assured them that Robert and Logan would be back as soon as he stabilized. Meanwhile at Baptist Hospital the doctors (and Robert) were busy trying to find out just what was wrong.

At approximately 8:00 p.m. Logan did stabilize! He was taken off the oxygen and Robert got to hold him and play with him. How special that bonding time was for Robert! God was answering our prayers, and our baby was going to be all right! Robert called me with joy in his voice to let me know that if Logan continued to improve they were coming back the next day!

I was sleeping peacefully at 4:00 a.m. Sunday morning when my nurse came to awaken me. Robert was calling to tell me that Logan's condition had worsened and I needed to get to Baptist Hospital as soon as my doctor would release me. Robert explained that the doctors at Bowman Gray were going to do a heart catheterization and were not sure that Logan was going to survive it. Surgery! And possibly DEATH! Now I was suddenly petrified. I got a quick release from the hospital, managed to throw some things in a suitcase at home, and hastily told Taylor good-bye. He wanted to know when Logan was coming home. I told him I didn't know and that Logan was sick. He might not come home for a long time, and he might not ever come home. I held him as we wept together. I promised him that he could stay at his best friend's house while we were gone and then I had to leave.

My mother drove me to Baptist Hospital. The trip seemed endless. As we traveled down a narrow, winding, two-lane mountain road to get to the main highway, we prayed and cried and prayed and cried. Why did Logan stabilize last night and have such a turn-about this morning? What was a heart catheterization, and why were the doctors doing it? I felt so out of control. If only he could hang on till we got there, everything would be all right. I couldn't do anything about it in the car 85 miles away. This wasn't happening to me – surely I was going to wake up from this bad dream. Yet, at the same time, I knew it was real.

When we arrived at the hospital, Phillip escorted us to the Neo-natal Intensive Care Unit (NICU). The cardiologist came to tell us that the surgery went well. They had videotaped it. He explained that Logan's heart did not have one of the channels through which the blood flowed back and forth. He described how he sent a tiny balloon up into Logan's heart through an artery in his leg and poked a hole through which the blood could better flow back and forth. He also explained that this was only a temporary measure.

In the NICU nursery, I noticed a small plastic bag with a lock of Logan's hair taped to his isolette and I quizzed my mother about it. She said that the nurses had to shave a tiny place on his head in order to hook up some of the monitors and they had saved his hair. I am very grateful that they had the foresight to do that, because now I treasure that lock of hair. It's the only tangible reminder I have of Logan.

The next several days at the hospital are a blur to me; I wish I had kept a journal. I know my mind was in a state of shock to cushion the events that were taking place around me. I can remember the success of the initial operation and the cardiologist telling us he felt that Logan was born with Hypoplastic Left Heart Syndrome (a condition in which a chamber of the left heart is missing and some valves are not formed correctly.) Learning this made us more fearful for our son's life.

The neo-natal heart surgeon was out of town and would not return until Tuesday. Later that day the cardiologist told us he felt Logan was not as serious as he had originally thought and that it just seemed his "plumbing" was messed up, but it was now working out its own flow pattern. He felt that there might not have to be any more surgery. We were ecstatic! Several of our friends were in the room with us, and they were praising God. In unity we offered a prayer of thanksgiving. The cardiologist even said he should have a relatively normal life. He cautioned us that he wanted the neo-natal heart surgeon to view the video of the surgery before he made a definite diagnosis. We expected to go home within the week.

A short while later as I stood by Logan's tiny bed, I felt him squeeze my finger, and even though he had trouble opening his eyes, I sensed he could see me. I took this to be an improvement. He seemed to already have a personality, calming down as I stroked him, and even smiling. He had quickly gained the love of his doctors and nurses. Everyone said he was a fighter.

On Tuesday I got to hold Logan! He was still all hooked up to the machines and the respirator and as a result he didn't like to be moved. As soon as he was in my arms though, he settled down to sleep peacefully. It was as if he knew that being in his mother's arms was where he should be. I sat close to his isolette, and rocked him for over an hour. I had ached to hold him, and now it felt so satisfying to have him with me. I sat there and cried with him in my arms. At last I was able to caress my baby. Oh, thank you God for this baby and for the miracles you are working out in his little life!

We finally got to meet the neo-natal heart surgeon. We were in high hopes of an optimistic diagnosis, but the news was devastating. After viewing the video, he concluded that Logan did indeed have Hypoplastic Left Heart Syndrome. We had several options. A heart transplant would be ideal. There were no donors readily available, and we had no clue as to where, how, and if we could get one. If we could, would that even be what we wanted to do? If we did nothing, he might die and the doctor assured us that would not be an unethical or morally bad decision. Thirdly, there were two surgical procedures he could perform.

Robert and I both felt that we just had to give Logan a chance. I felt a hole burning in my stomach – the worst feeling I had ever experienced in my life – and it wasn't going to end soon. Life-and-death decisions are not fun. We never thought we would have to decide the fate of one of our children. We agonized over this decision. After many questions and intense emotional struggle, we chose surgery. Logan had a seven in ten chance of surviving. I knew that with my family, friends and even strangers praying for him, Logan could beat those odds. He was scheduled for surgery the next day.

Wednesday, we got up early to see Logan off to surgery. When we arrived, the nurses were already preparing him and we had to stand back to allow them to work. With all the frantic movement going on around us, my mind and heart began to race. Would I ever see my son alive again? What would he be like after surgery? Could we really trust this doctor? I bent down to give him a hasty kiss. My lipstick was still on his little head as they rolled him down the hall. It's silly, but I felt like a part of me was going with him. We were allowed to go down the elevator and as far as the operating room doors with him. As they whisked him through the swinging doors, the anesthesiologist stopped long enough to tell us that she would take care of him. That was reassuring in the middle of all this trauma, but as we watched the doors swing shut, I broke down and cried.

The surgery started at 8:00 a.m. In the surgical waiting room with nothing to do, time seemed to stand still. Once during the morning the cardiologist came to give us a progress report. There had been some problem during the operation and Logan's heart had stopped. They got it started again and things seemed to be progressing as well as could be expected. He would return when they were finished. All we could do was wait and pray.

Around 1 p.m. both doctors returned. They were optimistic, and again called Logan "a little fighter." Things seemed to go well. Again we prayed a prayer of thanks.

We were allowed to go in to see Logan as soon as the nurses had him stabilized. The doctors had prepared us for what we were going to see, but it was still shocking to see our son limp, his skin gray and mottled. We were told this condition would improve as his circulation improved. The nurses were encouraging, saying that he had made it through the tough part. We spent the rest of the afternoon waiting for more encouraging signs. His little foot had been stuck so many times that I hurt for him. Although his feet were still bluish, his circulation did improve slightly, and he began to get some color back in his extremities. With this encouraging news we allowed ourselves to grab a bite to eat.

When we returned the nurses had changed shifts. Logan now had a male nurse. I usually waited for my husband to go with me to Logan's isolette, but this time I entered the nursery ahead of him. As I propped myself up on the stool next to Logan, I looked up at the nurse to get the latest developments. He simply said, "It doesn't look good, I don't think he's going to make it." A shock wave went through my body. I felt sick, panicky. All I wanted to do was get out of this horrible situation. I left the nursery numb.

My mother met me at the door of the nursery and immediately knew something was wrong. We went to the waiting room, and I tried to tell her what had happened. I couldn't talk; I didn't want to say the words. This wasn't happening! Robert returned from the nursery, and the nurse came to apologize for being so blunt.

I don't remember going back into the nursery after that. I wanted to remember my son alive, squeezing my finger, smiling through his respirator and opening his eyes to look at me. I didn't want to remember him still and limp and with unnatural skin color. He was such a pretty baby with blue eyes and long, dark brown hair. The realization that he might not survive crushed me. We had made such plans for him and his brother.

Nothing significant happened for several hours, and the nurses came to urge us to go and get some rest. They would call us if anything happened. Reluctantly, we left. Back at the hotel room, we prayed and cried. Sleep was nearly impossible. I think I felt closer to my husband at that time than at any other time because we were helping each other through a crisis that no one else could know. I needed him and was so afraid. Why was God letting this happen to our son? Hundreds of people were praying. My faith had been absolute that He would heal Logan and now He wasn't even letting him survive the surgery! Oh God, where are you? Though I felt abandoned, I came to realize that God was walking with us the whole time.

We continued to pray that night and managed to get some sleep. Early the next morning the phone rang. I couldn't answer it. When Robert picked it up, he was informed that we should come to the hospital. When we arrived, Robert hurried to the nursery; I couldn't bear to go. The situation was under God's control; I couldn't do a thing. The nurses told Robert that Logan's heart had stopped several times during the night and they had gotten it started again. They could keep on trying to do that until eventually it didn't work, or we could let him die more peacefully. What an incredible decision to have to make, but we wanted him to be as comfortable as possible.

Seven days after he was born, Logan went to spend eternity with our Savior. He died on his brother's fifth birthday. I felt let down; my faith for a miracle had been so strong. But my way was not God's way. We prayed a prayer of thanksgiving that God had accepted Logan into His Kingdom. It was all over and Logan was finally free from disease, the wires, and the monitors.

Our pastor came and a little later the surgeon arrived. He explained he had been with Logan earlier that morning and didn't know why he had taken a turn for the worse. He also wanted to ask us about an autopsy. This was unbearable, and he knew it, judging by the anguish showing on his face. He explained that Logan could help him learn what had gone wrong with the surgery, and perhaps he would be able to improve the procedure. This decision was heart-wrenching. How could we possibly make a decision like that feeling as we did? Yet, we knew that if there was a chance that it would help other little babies, there was no choice. After all, we knew that Logan was not in that body right now, but peacefully in Heaven. We finally agreed, asking them to stay within certain limits.

Before we left the hospital that day, Robert went in to the nursery one last time to hold our son and to say good-bye for both of us. The nurses placed a rocking chair behind a screen and it was there that he spent a long time agonizing over the loss of our little boy and letting out his emotions.

We left the hospital and drove to the funeral home to make arrangements and select a casket. The funeral was to be the next day. I was numb and couldn't believe this was happening to us. Thankfully, Robert was able to make the decisions. We drove to the cemetery to choose a plot. Someone had already come and paid for it. To this day we don't know who it was.

When we got home, I couldn't bear going through the door we normally use where I would be faced with the empty crib. We used the front door instead. Entering the bedroom later, I found that my friends had already taken the crib and baby things away. I was extremely grateful that I didn't have to deal with that. Going to the window and looking out, I broke down and cried. How was I going to make it? I felt like the rug had been jerked out from under me. I had no control over anything. I couldn't help asking God, "Why?"

Later that night we had to tell Taylor. We sensed that he had many questions, but just didn't know what to ask. He was greatly distressed and said, "I didn't even get to see him!" Since he had seen him in the hospital, we weren't sure what he meant. He explained "I didn't get to see his back." It occurred to me that children want to touch and feel all of what is special to them and he didn't get to do that. He cried, "It's just not fair, it's just not fair!" My feelings exactly. Taylor cried himself to sleep that night.

The next day my parents encouraged me to go to the funeral home and visit Logan one last time. I was reluctant, but when my mother suggested that later in life I might wish I had gone, I realized she was right. This was the most agonizing thing I had ever had to do. Robert went with me. The lady at the home was caring and knew how to handle the situation. However, I couldn't stay in his room long; I still wanted to remember him alive; looking at me, squeezing my finger. He seemed so wise and peaceful lying in his little casket; as if he knew why all this had happened. He was dressed in a little blue outfit with a train design on it. One of our closest friends had given it to him the day he was born. The little white bunny Taylor had given him was placed beside him. Tearfully leaving his body, we sat in another room and cried and cried and cried uncontrollably.

Later, as the limousine was taking us to the cemetery, it began to sprinkle. Our pastor warned us that the little family service we had felt was appropriate had turned into a much larger gathering. He was right. Many, many friends were there to share with us in our time of grief.

It was such a fulfilling service. Our pastor said that Logan had touched many lives already — that all of us had been made more aware of the suffering of children and we each clutched the significant people in our lives more dearly because of the events of the week. He said that even though Logan lived a short life, it was a complete life. Life's completeness is never measured by temporal calculations of time punctuated by days and years. Though our sorrow pushes us at this point with questions about "fullness of life," we must know that God always and only breathes wholeness into what He creates. God seems to be perfectly willing to use "biological failure" for the sake of molding us into His completeness. He also said that Logan was a full human being, who, with a limited heart, had the whole heart of God invested in him and the whole heart of many others involved in his life.

The next day as I waited for Robert to pick up some dry-cleaning, a friend spotted our car and walked over to me and said, "Well, when are you going to have that baby anyway?" He hadn't heard! I was devastated. What was I going to say to him? Upon learning the news, he just walked away from the car without a word. I felt sorry for him, but I didn't want to have to recount the details of the past week again. So we left the next day with Phillip's family to spend time away at their beach house.

On the beach there were two boys about five years apart in age playing together. I couldn't help thinking over and over again how Taylor and Logan would have been playing like that in a few years and now I would never be able to see them together.

In the days that followed, our friends continued to surround us with their love and help us in many ways. They would talk about Logan, ask questions, and let me talk about him. One of my biggest fears was that no one would remember him. It still feels good to hear people say his name.

We were also directed to meaningful scriptures. One of the special ones was II Samuel 12:15-23. David's son fell sick and died seven days later, even after the elders of his household tried to raise him up from his sickness. I could relate to that! The verse that really comforted me was the last one in which David said, "I shall go to him, but he will not return to me." I know that means Logan will be there in Heaven and will recognize us when we see him again. Another verse that gives me hope is I Corinthians 13:12 which speaks of "when the perfect comes" (i.e. when we are perfected in Heaven); it says, **"For now we see in a mirror dimly, but then face to face; now I know in part, but then I shall know fully just as I also have been fully known."**

In the months that followed I still questioned God. I wondered if Logan's death happened because of something I had done. Was it because I had often joked about how I was going to manage two children and a business at the same time? Was I being punished for something? How could God let a little baby go through surgery and then watch him die? How could we think that Logan was going to be all right, only to lose him? How could He let my body go through childbirth and not have anything to show for it?

It helped me immensely to read Isaiah 55:8-9. These verses say that God's thoughts are not our thoughts; His ways are higher than our ways and His thoughts higher than our thoughts. My way was for God to perform a miracle with Logan, but I must trust God that His way is the perfect way. I also know that God set Logan apart, even while he was in my womb, for His glory (Galatians 1:15).

About three months after Logan was born, Robert accepted a new job in Charlotte, North Carolina. After we moved, we visited various churches and decided to join Calvary Church. There I met several women who had also lost babies and were getting together to share experiences. Since we were all Christians, we could express our questions and our feelings in light of the fact that God was Sovereign. It was comforting to know other people who were going through the same sort of experiences and questions that we were.

We would support each other on special occasions, and be there for each other through difficult times.

Another thing that many of us in the support group did was to start "scrap" books. Anything that related to our babies including pictures, birth certificates, articles, funerals, their obituaries, etc., went into their special book. I was fortunate to be able to include Logan's lock of hair.

About six months after Logan was born I got involved in a Bible study class. In this class we focused on how to take in the very principles you need in order to live a Christian life. I found a lot of the answers to my questions about God. I realized that even though I may see a lot of good that has come from Logan's birth and death, I may not ever know the meaning or all the reasons why he died. After all, the scope of my mind is so limited compared to God's. I know that God allowed this to happen to Logan (for whatever reason) and He will work it all out for good.

I still look at other children Logan's age and wonder what he would have been like. But now I can smile thinking of him playing in heaven, perhaps with some of my friends' sons and daughters.

One year after Logan's birth, I became pregnant for the fourth time. We were thrilled, yet so afraid. We had been through genetic counseling and knew that while we had a one percent chance (normal) of a heart defect with Logan, our chances were doubled with this baby. Two percent doesn't sound like very much until you have been that one percent statistic. As my pregnancy developed, my obstetrician sent us to a prenatal heart specialist for further testing at sixteen weeks. Although we knew that there would be no way that we would terminate this pregnancy, we wanted to be prepared.

The day we drove to the specialist, we were bathed in prayer and felt fairly confident. Still, on the examining table I feared the worst. As the doctor looked at the blobs on the screen that reflected our baby, she reassured us that she could indeed see four chambers of the heart. We cried for joy.

We were blessed with a healthy baby girl. The first week of her life was shaky for us since she was in a home incubator for several days because of severe jaundice. This brought back memories of Logan's stay in the isolette. I often feared God would take this baby, too. This time we had a happier ending. Adrienne is a healthy, happy little girl and as active as any child could be.

Robert and I still talk about Logan frequently. We continue to shed tears over him; but we trust God, knowing that someday we shall be with our son again, forever, in a place where Logan has been given a glorious new body (Philippians 3:21), where he is whole and healthy, where he can run and play, and where his Heavenly Father is watching over him.

We look forward to the time when **"He will swallow up death for all time, and the Lord God will wipe tears away from all faces" (Isaiah 25:8a).**

Remarks from Logan's funeral...

"As Logan sits in the presence of God, we can dare live on.
Blessed with the gift of Logan,
Comforted by Christ in our grief,
Our hearts plumbed to deeper levels,
Our souls enriched, informed, strengthened."

Dr. Steven Carreker
First Baptist Church of Boone, North Carolina

LINDSEY: OUR LITTLE ROSEBUD

By Susie Norton

"And those who know Thy name will put their trust in Thee; for Thou, O Lord, hast not forsaken those who seek Thee" (Psalm 9:10). "And after you have suffered for a little while, the God of all grace, who called you to His eternal glory in Christ, will Himself perfect, confirm, strengthen and establish you" (I Peter 5:10).

L indsey would be almost 10 months old now as I begin to write her story. My heart still aches for her, and I still long to hold her in my arms. I will always miss her, but feel a great peace knowing that she is with our Heavenly Father and that I will be with her again (I Thessalonians 4:16-18). I think about her every day and wonder what life with her would have been like. How would she look? Would she be trying to walk? Would she be sleeping through the night yet? How much happiness and joy would she have brought to our lives? These questions and others have no answers. Her little life was shortened to 26 wonderful, joyous, anxious hours. She was like a precious little rosebud who came into our lives, and then, before she could fully bloom, was taken from us. This is her story; a story of God's love, grace, and provision in the midst of devastating heartache.

Her story actually begins, I believe, several months before her conception. I was involved in a Bible study on the book of John and reflecting on the verse: **"I am the true vine, and my Father is the vinedresser. Every branch in Me that does not bear fruit, He takes away; and every branch that bears fruit, He prunes it, that it may bear more fruit ... abide in Me" (John 15:1-4).**

Although I had become a Christian eleven years earlier, my Christian walk had been careful and safe. It wasn't that I didn't desire a deeper commitment, but I feared the trials that might come my way, and really was busy just keeping up with my daily activities. After reading the verse in John, I prayed for God to do what pruning He felt necessary for me, to mold me as He willed, so that I might be more conformed to Christ's image and more useful to Him here on earth.

In April I learned I was pregnant. What a surprise! I was thrilled and nervous at the same time. Here I was at 41, the mother of an 11-year-old son, Bryan, and an 8-year-old daughter, Rachel. What would it be like to begin again with a new little one? And yet, I had always secretly wanted one more child, and felt this was the beginning of an unexpected but exciting journey. My husband, Harry, was cautiously happy about the news. Bryan and Rachel were ecstatic. They had often asked for a new brother or sister, and now had a good time debating about the baby's sex and name. My constant prayer was for God's blessing upon this child, and that he be healthy and normal. I would learn that God's answer to prayer is not always as we request, and that His answer can be very hard to understand.

The first trimester went well with practically no nausea – a first for me. Newer medical technology allowed me to hear the baby's heartbeat at two months. It sounded strong and wonderful. Because of my age, I desired an amniocentesis mostly for reassurance that the baby was well. Meanwhile, we began remodeling our home to give us added space for the baby. I bought maternity clothes and happily settled into the pregnancy.

The morning of July 5th, I went alone to the Women's Center for the amniocentesis. Harry remained at home with Bryan and Rachel at my request. I was anxious about the procedure itself, but had no concerns about the results. At the center, after a consultation with a genetics counselor, I was taken to a room for the test. As the baby's head came into view on the ultrasound screen, I became very excited and awed at being able to see my little child so early in its development. The technician then moved the wand down to the front of the head. She hesitated when two large black areas of fluid appeared at each side of the baby's neck. "Cystic hygroma," she called it. More dark fluid appeared to surround the lining of the baby's lungs. "Pleural effusion. Not a good sign." The technician left the room, and returned several minutes later with the genetics counselor. I went numb as she explained that these black areas of lymphatic fluid generally indicate a chromosomal abnormality, though only the results of the amniocentesis could confirm this. The doctor arrived to do the procedure and confirmed these preliminary findings, saying the condition appeared, on a scale of moderate to severe, to be lethal. He felt the baby could possibly die at any time during the pregnancy. The ultrasound also indicated a possible two-chamber heart. Everyone was compassionate and caring, but nothing helped as a numbing fog of shock and disbelief settled on me. Our unborn baby had severe problems. We had to wait two weeks to find out exactly what they were. But whatever they were, death suddenly and ominously threatened our tiny baby's life.

I somehow managed to drive home. Harry and I talked alone. He was as distressed as I was, and became a strong support for me for many long months. With discomfort from the test, I rested in bed the remainder of the day, reading Psalms, crying, and praying that God would reach His hand down to touch and heal my baby.

The Lord's wonderful timing and care began at this point. Friends called about the test and began praying for us. The sermon at church the following Sunday was entitled "Stork Reality" and was based on Psalm 139:13-16. This was the first time I had ever noticed these Scripture verses:

"For Thou didst form my inward parts;
Thou didst weave me in my mother's womb.
I will give thanks to Thee, for I am fearfully and wonderfully made;
Wonderful are Thy works, and my soul knows it very well.
My frame was not hidden from Thee, when I was made in secret,
And skillfully wrought in the depths of the earth.
Thine eyes have seen my unformed substance;
and in Thy book they were all written,
The days that were ordained for me, when as yet there was not one of them."

A measure of peace came over me. In spite of my sorrow, I knew that God – my Sovereign Father – was in control. He was weaving this baby as He ordained it should be. Whatever was happening, He had a reason and a purpose for it. In whatever He was allowing to come our way, I knew He would be there with us, guiding us, caring for us, comforting us.

Twelve days later we made an appointment to discuss the results of the test with one of the doctors. The nurse explained that the test showed the baby had a chromosomal abnormality called Trisomy 18, but she could tell me nothing else. I later learned my baby was a little girl. It was a sadly sweet moment. I found out that Trisomy 18 babies have an extra chromosome, with a total of 47 instead of the normal 46. The extra 18th chromosome pulls the normal development of the baby out of whack, and leads to many problems. Ninety-nine percent of these babies miscarry early. Of those who do go full term, most have heart problems, and some very distinct physical characteristics as well as profound mental retardation. Most of these babies live only a few days to several months. Their care is very difficult, though the babies themselves seem to have happy, sweet dispositions.

The news was devastating. I could cope with it only by knowing that God was in charge and He Himself was weaving Lindsey in my womb for a reason. Otherwise, everything seemed so senseless. A part of me felt this was a joke being played on me, that I was being teased. Here I was, so excited about being given the third child I had always wanted, and suddenly she was being snatched back. She might die any day or survive to her due date, five months later. At birth, she could die immediately or live maybe a short while. Harry and I were overwhelmed. The doctor told us that with such news, five out of six couples would terminate the pregnancy at this point. As hopeless as the situation appeared, and unbearable as the next five months looked, abortion was not a consideration. She was our child, and we could not end her life, regardless of what her problems were. The days that were ordained for her were in the Lord's hands, not ours. We would protect her and give her every chance possible. We would trust the Lord for His plan and purpose for her life.

We had to tell Bryan and Rachel. We gathered them in the family room with us that evening after the talk with doctor, and told them that their baby sister had a chromosomal problem and apparently a two chamber heart, and most likely she would not live long, if at all, once she was born. Rachel burst into tears and sobbed for two hours. Bryan quietly walked away without a word, feeling very vulnerable. To him, this was something that happened to other people, not to his loved ones. They each handled their grief in their own ways and we drew close together as a family in the months that followed.

I began feeling emotionally torn. Lindsey was kicking now. Every part of me wanted to love her. I found myself enjoying all her movements and I even proudly put her ultrasound picture up in the kitchen to show everyone how "cute" she was. At the same time, I fiercely tried to stay detached; to pretend that there was no baby, that my waistline was just getting thick, that nothing in our lives had changed. It was too painful to think of falling in love with this child, knowing she would most likely die soon after birth. Numbness set in. Friends, acquaintances, and strangers made the usual friendly comments to the "mother-to-be." We told only people closest to us about Lindsey and those we would see frequently.

The monthly checkups at the doctor's office were very difficult. Seeing the happily expectant moms and couples, some with children, all looking forward to their new baby's arrival became a real ordeal for me. The doctors were kind but mostly very businesslike. One doctor actually lectured me for wasting the time, money, and lab work to have another ultrasound done of the baby's heart at 28 weeks. With such a poor prognosis, he felt it was not worth the trouble or expense. That was the only time I cried at the doctor's office. He walked out on me. The nurses never indicated they were aware of my situation and simply did their job. Near my due date, I learned they were all aware of the prognosis, but never gave a comforting word.

Harry made tentative funeral arrangements preferring to do it alone to spare me the trauma. We felt some measure of control by doing what little we could to prepare for Lindsey's apparently inevitable death.

Physically, the pregnancy was more difficult than my two previous ones, perhaps due to the combination of age and stress. As my due date approached, I became more and more withdrawn, and preferred to stay at home, quietly preparing for Christmas. (This was the only year I have ever been completely finished with Christmas preparation – except for the tree – a month ahead!)

The second ultrasound of Lindsey's heart showed severe deformity, with apparently two chambers and a very narrow artery leading to the lungs. She would likely die from congestive heart failure within minutes after birth. By now, Harry and I were past being shocked. We simply prayed that we would have time to get to know her and that she would not suffer. In subsequent checkups at the doctor's office, it was difficult to believe that Lindsey's heart was so malformed when it sounded so healthy and normal.

In spite of the trying circumstances surrounding us, the Lord gave us the strength to face each day. He promises us the victory over trials if we will hold fast to our faith and keep our eyes fastened firmly on Him and not on the circumstances or ourselves. I finally truly understood my baptismal verse: **"Do not fear, for I am with you; Do not anxiously look about you, for I am your God. I will strengthen you, surely I will help you, Surely I will uphold you with My righteous right hand"** (Isaiah 41:10).

As long as I trusted Him, I was fine. As soon as I looked at what was happening and at myself, I fell apart. Prayer and the Psalms became my constant companions. The support, encouragement, prayers, and notes from friends and even strangers were a joy to both Harry and me. I still prayed for healing for Lindsey, but ultimately, that God's will would be done.

I wanted this pregnancy to be an effective Christian witness to those I met. Neighbors and others indicated an abortion would have been an easier route to follow. As a Christian, I could not abort my baby. However, I could not allow myself to walk around with a long and sad face. Such an attitude would only reinforce their thoughts of how foolish it was to allow myself to suffer so needlessly when, in their eyes, there was a better alternative. I wanted the world to know that, through Christ, there can be victory over even the most devastating experiences. The Lord gave me such conviction that trusting Him was the right thing to do, I felt a tremendous peace. I pray that my life reflected the reassuring peace which sustained me during this time.

The "Footprints" poem tells us that God is always by our side in our Christian walk and that He carries us through the hardest times. We cannot plan His carrying us. It happens at the moment and time we need Him.

Three days before Lindsey was born, events and circumstances began falling perfectly into place, even though at the time I was not aware this was happening. God began carrying us through, arranging our lives so we wouldn't have to worry. I prepared all of Rachel's school supplies for Monday as soon as she came home from school on Friday instead of waiting until Sunday evening as I usually did. I organized the house. Two weeks were left before Lindsey's due date, but on Sunday I started experiencing fairly regular contractions. Since these had been occurring occasionally for months, I was not too concerned. My total loss of appetite seemed to indicate some sort of a change, though. We had just finished the last of our Christmas preparations. A friend of Rachel's came to play unexpectedly and we invited her to spend the night. Because I was not experiencing pain we didn't leave for the hospital, even though the contractions had been coming at two to three minute intervals for several hours. We took Bryan to a friend's house at 10:00 p.m. just in case I really was in labor. (I had had a similar episode of false labor a month earlier, had spent 6 hours in the hospital before being sent home, and did not care to make another dry run.) Still there was no pain. Finally, with bags packed, we went to bed at 11 p.m. As I prayed for a sign that this truly was labor, my water broke. We went to the hospital. Fifty-five difficult minutes after we arrived, Lindsey was born.

It's interesting what a person notices at such times. As the doctor lifted her up and handed her to the neonatologist, I saw that her umbilical cord did not look normal but appeared swollen and distended. I felt this was God's way of showing me that He had chosen not to heal her. After 30 minutes, the neonatologist tentatively confirmed the diagnosis of Trisomy 18. A lab culture verified this several days later.

I asked to hold her. There is no greater joy than holding your newborn baby. All the months of heartache dissolved as she was placed in my arms. She was wonderful to me. I held her close, and never wanted to let go. However, she was breathing with some difficulty and I knew she needed to go to ICU and be placed on oxygen. An hour later, I was wheeled to her side and Harry and I held our precious daughter again. Her nasal passages were blocked and she could only breathe through her mouth. A tube ran into her mouth and down to her stomach. An IV was placed in her arm. Electrodes were taped to her chest to monitor her heart and breathing rate. Large machines towered over the head of her bassinet, reading out her vital signs. She was stable. Her heart was pumping well. She did not even need extra oxygen. Harry and I felt encouraged. Perhaps she would do much better than the doctors had anticipated.

The following morning she was stable enough that the pediatrician mentioned the possibility of her going home. My hopes rose. Then 12 hours after she was born, she had her first attack of apnea. Her breathing nearly stopped for several minutes. Then just as suddenly, it returned to normal. She wasn't on a respirator; we had asked for no extraordinary measures to be taken to sustain her life. She was truly in the Lord's hands. Harry brought Bryan and Rachel to see Lindsey that afternoon. We felt it was important for them to hold her and get to know her. She had another spell of apnea in Bryan's arms.

We all watched helplessly but again she recovered and seemed fine.

My brother and his wife came and were able to hold her. Another attack of apnea came and passed. It became apparent that Lindsey was on the decline. Harry's mom flew up from Texas to see her. Lindsey began crying for the first time. This was not the lusty cry of a healthy newborn but sounded more like the plaintive cry of a little kitten. I was distressed. She seemed to be uncomfortable and the nurse gave her a little morphine to stop any pain.

Just after 8 p.m., a call came to my room from ICU to hurry down; Lindsey was not doing well. She again recovered by the time I got to her side and I held her for the next two hours. The apnea occurred more frequently. She would stop breathing, go into a trance, and her arms would stiffen. The nurse said the stiffened arms indicated brain damage. I was denying to myself how serious she was, that she was slowly dying. I rocked her and rubbed her feet and held her hands. The skin on her legs was dry and the nurse gave me some lotion to rub on them. It was such a small thing to do and yet, it was the only thing I ever did to care for her. I will always cherish the memory. It was during these two hours alone with her that I really bonded with her. By 10:30 p.m., I was exhausted. The nurse begged me to get some sleep and said they would call if they needed me to come. I reluctantly went, only because I was afraid of falling asleep with her in my arms and dropping her. I would not see her alive again.

At 1 a.m. on December 11th I awoke and called ICU. Lindsey was fine, they said. At 2 a.m., ICU called to tell me Lindsey was not doing well. I hurried down, put on my gown, scrubbed my hands, and went to her, only to find she had just died! I stared in utter shock and horror as she was placed on the bed from the nurse's arms while the doctor listened with his stethoscope and said she was gone. I was frozen. The nurse took Lindsey and led me to a small private room and placed her in my arms and left us alone. I cried. I held her. I kissed her. I undressed her and looked at her whole little self for the first time. The nurse came and I had her remove all the tubes and electrodes. I held her more and told her I loved her. I felt the warmth slowly leave her body. She looked so peaceful. Her struggle was over. For that I was thankful. Perhaps my not being there to hold her as she died was God's way of sparing me the agony of watching the numbers on the machines as they dropped to zero. I'll never know. I hope she knew how much she was loved.

Harry came and held her and told her good-bye. We gave her back to the nurse and quietly went back to my room and tried to fall asleep in each other's arms until the morning. It was all over. The next day we bought a little outfit for Lindsey's burial. It was the one thing we did together for her. Though it was a difficult task it brought us a small measure of comfort to have done this for her.

The day of the funeral was beautiful and warm, with a slight breeze blowing. We again said good-bye to Lindsey in her casket. So many people came to her funeral. My parents and sister, Harry's mom and another lifelong friend came a great distance to attend. We were so encouraged and comforted by everyone's coming. At one point during the service, sitting there under the tent, I noticed how bright and beautiful the day was and suddenly felt the presence of the Lord surrounding me with His most loving, comforting, reassuring presence. I will never forget the moment or the feeling of being so uplifted and surrounded by His love. He seemed to be telling me that He knew our pain, that He was there with us just as He had been throughout the pregnancy, and would continue to be in the many long months ahead.

For the first weeks after Lindsey's death, I could barely function. My arms ached so desperately and I couldn't fill them. My heart was more than broken, it was shattered. I endured all the postpartum changes that occur normally after a pregnancy: the hormonal fluctuations, my milk coming in – all painful reminders of our loss. Normally there is a reward to make it all worthwhile – a precious life. We did not have our baby. It didn't seem fair. Harry was given time off from work to help care for the family. Slowly the pain settled down. I still remember the day three or four weeks after the funeral when I actually felt almost normal for an entire morning before succumbing again to the heaviness of my grief.

The many cards, phone calls, visits, and meals that friends and family provided in those early weeks sustained us. Listening to my "praise tapes" helped keep my focus on God. I stayed in withdrawal for many months. It was difficult to interact with people when I felt so "out of sync" with them and life in general. Grieving is a long, hard process. I still struggle with it every day. As time slowly heals the pain, I try being more involved with people and activities. I still find it difficult when I see pregnant women, tiny infants and baby girls about Lindsey's age. Some days, they seem to be everywhere.

I am so thankful God gave us 26 hours to hold and get to know Lindsey. Those were precious hours that made the previous five months all worthwhile. We have never regretted our decision to continue the pregnancy and not terminate it. Though our dreams for our baby never will come to pass, we have some wonderful and precious memories that will stay in our hearts forever. On days when the loneliness seems especially overwhelming, I ask the Lord if He would just let her know that we love and miss her and always think about her.

Romans 8:28 tells us that **"God causes all things to work together for good to those who love God, to those who are called according to His purpose."** I believe this is true and pray that God will use Lindsey's life and death in some way to touch and help others. Just as the Lord used this experience to draw me close to Himself, I pray you also will be drawn close to Him and find peace and comfort, no matter what difficulty you're going through. To God be the glory.

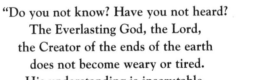

"Do you not know? Have you not heard?
The Everlasting God, the Lord,
the Creator of the ends of the earth
does not become weary or tired.
His understanding is inscrutable.
He gives strength to the weary, and to him who lacks might,
He increases power."
Isaiah 40:28-29

WHEN THERE ARE NO ANSWERS

by Jill Thigpen

Sometimes in this world things happen and there are no answers to the question, "Why?" I know because I began looking for that answer when our daughter Haley was stillborn. I thought I could not live to see another day. I felt an indescribable loneliness and hurt. The hardest part was trying to understand why God allowed this to happen.

Her death was totally unexpected. Her movement stopped and an ultrasound confirmed our biggest fear. Our baby had died in utero. After twelve and a half hours of difficult labor, our baby was delivered. She looked perfect and beautiful, like a little angel. My husband named her Haley, taken from an angel's halo. Our doctors and nurses were gentle and sensitive. They gave us privacy to hold our daughter and begin to make plans. Because she was delivered late in the night, none of our family was able to see or hold her. Then we went home with empty arms and heavy hearts. We buried our daughter in a special part of a cemetery set aside just for infants. Her marker says "In Jesus' Arms," which is how we feel. She went from our arms to our Savior's arms.

The autopsy found no cause of death and our doctors encouraged us, so I became pregnant again almost right away. Looking back I think it helped me deal with the loss of our first child, but I also became very fearful. I visited Haley's grave each week; then, as I got further along in this second pregnancy, my visits became less frequent. I was afraid to face death and I thought if I didn't go to the cemetery, her death would seem less real.

From the time I found out I was pregnant the second time, everyone I knew, and many people I didn't know, were praying for this unborn child and us. Through the death of our daughter we discovered that my blood type and my husband's blood type were incompatible. Although the autopsy report did not say this was the cause of our daughter's death, the doctors then knew how to treat this second pregnancy. My husband and I began weekly trips to Chapel Hill, North Carolina to see a specialist. Through a procedure called fetal blood sampling, whereby a needle passes through the mother's stomach and amniotic sac and into the umbilical cord to withdraw a sampling of the baby's blood, it was discovered that my blood type and the baby's blood type were different. My blood was unable to give the baby proper nourishment and, therefore, was causing the baby to become anemic.

My doctor at Chapel Hill treated this condition with bi-monthly in utero blood transfusions - blood compatible with the baby's was slowly passed into the umbilical cord.

Each transfusion would supply the baby with enough nourishment until the next transfusion. I dreaded our trips to Chapel Hill because the procedure was very painful and also put the baby at risk. But each visit brought us closer to the time our baby would be born.

I was so afraid to hope for the future, but I honestly thought that God was working a miracle in our lives and for our baby. I felt God was trying to teach us something through the death of Haley and, whatever the lesson was, I would learn it without having to suffer another loss. In my mind I justified Haley's death because through it the doctors learned how to treat our next baby. We were praying so hard, as were our friends and family. I felt sure we would get to bring this second baby home. An ultrasound revealed our baby was a boy, so we named him Garrett Ezekiel, which means "our brave warrior whom the Lord strengthens." As we watched him fight for his life every day, the name seemed to fit our son perfectly.

During our last transfusion, our baby's heart rate dropped. Though I could not see what was going on, I instinctively knew something was wrong. My husband, who stayed by my head, held my hand, and talked to me throughout each operation, told me one of the doctors had left the room. Then I knew something was terribly wrong. My doctor told me that in order to try to save our baby, they would have to do an emergency C-section. Within seconds the operating room was filled with doctors and nurses. My husband was pushed out of the operating room and a nurse began hooking me up to all sorts of machines. I was so afraid. I remember telling the nurse, "Please don't let my baby die!" Within six minutes our son, Garrett Ezekiel, was born. The doctors were able to stabilize him and move him to the neonatal intensive care unit. As soon as I came out of recovery, the nurses took my husband and me into the ICU to see our son for the first time. He was under warm lights and had tubes running in and out of him. But as I looked at his tiny, helpless body I was filled with such love and peace. He was such a miracle. The nurses carefully laid him in my arms. He was so beautiful – absolutely perfect. I don't know how long I held him, but I have every detail etched in my mind. The doctors told us he was a very sick little boy, but they would do everything they could to help him.

I was taken to my room where I began to doze due to the anesthesia. I awoke with a start when the neonatal doctor came into my room. He didn't have to say a word; we knew Garrett had died. Our beautiful little boy, for whom we had fought so hard, lived four short hours before joining his sister in heaven. Another part of me died that day too.

Not long after the doctor told us our son had died, the nurse brought Garrett into the room and we held him for a long time. My brother and his wife, who live in Chapel Hill, came. They held Garrett and held us as we cried over our second loss. Why? Why did the Lord find it necessary to allow our second child to die? I struggled to find an answer.

Because no one else in our family had seen our daughter, it was extremely important to me that my mom and dad see their grandson. Early the next morning, my parents and our ten-year-old son, Ricky (my husband's natural son, whom I had adopted), came to the hospital. The social worker at the hospital brought Garrett back to us. His little body was cold, but he still looked so pretty and sweet. It was important to us for our family to see

Garrett. I think Ricky needed to be a part of this to help him understand that he had a brother. Not having seen Haley, it was easy to pretend she never existed. But both Haley and Garrett were real; they were members of our family and I wanted everyone to remember them.

I stayed in the hospital for five days. During this time the nurses and doctors were wonderful. They cried with us, listened to us, and helped us make arrangements to take Garrett back to Charlotte, North Carolina where we lived. They gave us the support we needed to get us through those first dreadful days.

Garrett was buried near his sister. Those who had prayed for him attended the graveside service. Then I went home to recuperate from the surgery and to begin healing emotionally. It wasn't easy. Physically, I felt better in a few weeks, but emotionally and spiritually, I was empty. The pieces did not fit together to make sense out of the past year.

Did any of my questions have answers? Some did, but most did not. I knew my children were in heaven and, that given a choice, they wouldn't come back to live on this earth. I knew that one day I would be reunited with my children in heaven. Yet, I wanted them here and now, and I just plain hurt. My heart was broken and I felt an endless emptiness. Without my family, friends, and a God who promised to take care of me, I know I could never have made it through those long days, weeks, and months.

Through these experiences I have learned a lot about life, death, and myself. Life is so precious and each child is a miracle. I have learned that no matter what a person has been through before, he/she cannot be prepared to lose a loved one. Yet the Lord promises to be with us, and He strengthened me and upheld me during the many times I felt alone and lonely.

Do I still have questions? Every day. There will never be a good enough answer to why both of my children died. No one on this earth can answer these questions. Only God can, and I know He'll answer them when I meet Him face to face.

I still miss my children and I think of them so often. Nothing will ever take away the pain of losing them. The pain brings memories of my daughter and my son, and that's all I have of them. I want to remember their movement within my womb and their tiny faces when I first laid eyes on them. Recalling these things reminds me of how precious and perfect we are in God's sight.

As I've reflected on the two beautiful children God gave us, but didn't let us keep, I was inspired to memorialize them in a poem. It has helped to capture my feelings for them – my longing to see them one day.

For My Precious Children
I wondered who you'd look like
Maybe me, perhaps Dad;
I wondered what your future held,
A future you never had.
I never looked into your eyes
Or held your tiny hand;

Now you play on streets of gold
In God's heavenly land.
Why you're no longer here
I just can't understand,
But I know I'll recognize you
In God's heavenly land.
I'll know your precious voice,
I'll hug you, oh, so near;
My heart will be complete again
I'll thank God He brought you here.

God kept us close to Him and continued to give us a strong desire for another child. Our doctors advised us not to try again because we would face the same problems. So we began to look into adoption.

Through our minister we became aware of a young woman who was seeking adoptive parents for her unborn child. We prayerfully submitted a profile of our family and waited. One special day we received a phone call from our minister. The woman wanted us to have her baby. She said she wanted to help ease our pain with the loss of our two babies by giving us her child. Her due date was seven days away. We began to prepare the nursery for the third time. We were excited, scared, and filled with anticipation. There was always the chance that the woman would change her mind even up to ninety days after the birth of the baby. Deciding to put these fears behind us, we placed our trust in God and waited for the baby's birth. Shortly thereafter, our son, Addison Robert, was born. When the young woman was in labor, we were called to the hospital. We saw Addison when he was ten minutes old and was being weighed and measured. I could not have been more joyful and thankful than when I held him for the first time. We were so grateful to this birth mother and conveyed our thanks through her counselor, since we did not meet her. What a special woman she is to have given us such a gift. We continue to thank God for her daily. No one could have given us a gift greater than the privilege of raising and loving this child.

We brought Addison home when he was two days old. Those first weeks were a blur. I still couldn't believe this tiny child was mine. He felt so good in my arms, and I began to feel the rawness of my pain start to mellow. The nursery was no longer a sad room, but my favorite room in the house. It was filled with love and life.

As I watch Addison grow and develop each day, I marvel at what a miracle it is that he belongs to us. What a blessing he is to every member of my family. He makes me realize each day how much God loves us to have sent us this precious child.

Yes, God is faithful and He answers our prayers, although not always the way we think He will. Looking back, I can see God's hand in every detail surrounding the deaths of Haley and Garrett and the adoption of Addison. He has given me strength and peace. He has led me to new friends and made me more sensitive to the needs of others. Because of Haley and Garrett I look forward to the second coming of Christ with greater anticipation. I have two very special little children waiting for me. When that day comes, I know I will feel whole again.

My Prayer to God

Keep me strong, help me to stand
Support me with Your loving hand
Hold me tight, O Lord, I pray
Guide me through another day.
Heal my heart and wipe my tears
Take away my pain and fears
Give me peace, O Lord, I pray
Guide me through another day.
Show me how to share a smile
Push me to go the extra mile
Let me love, O Lord, I pray
Those who are hurting every day.
- Jill Thigpen -

PART IV
YOUR OWN
PERSONAL STORY

"For He will give His angels charge
concerning you, to guard you in all
your ways." Psalm 91:11

MY PERSONAL STORY

APPENDIX

APPENDIX I

SOMEONE CARES FOR YOU

Scripture Verses For Comfort

Lamentations 3:21-23

"This I recall to my mind, therefore I have hope. The Lord's lovingkindnesses indeed never cease, for His compassions never fail, they are new every morning; great is thy faithfulness."

I Corinthians 10:13

"No temptation has overtaken you but such as is common to man; and God is faithful, who will not allow you to be tempted beyond what you are able, but with the temptation will provide the way of escape also, that you may be able to endure it."

Proverbs 3:5-6

"Trust in the Lord with all your heart, and do not lean on your own understanding. In all your ways acknowledge Him, and he will make your paths straight."

Joshua 1:9

"Have I not commanded you? Be strong and courageous! Do not tremble or be dismayed, for the Lord your God is with you wherever you go."

Psalm 27:13-14

"I would have despaired unless I had believed that I would see the goodness of the Lord in the land of the living. Wait for the Lord; be strong, and let your heart take courage; yes, wait for the Lord."

II Corinthians 1:3-4

"Blessed be the God and Father of our Lord Jesus Christ, the Father of mercies and God of all comfort; who comforts us in all our affliction so that we may be able to comfort those who are in any affliction with the comfort with which we ourselves are comforted by God. For just as the sufferings of Christ are ours in abundance, so also our comfort is abundant through Christ."

Philippians 4:13

"I can do all things through Him who strengthens me."

Isaiah 41:10

"Do not fear, for I am with you; do not anxiously look about you, for I am your God. I will strengthen you, surely I will help you, surely I will uphold you with my righteous right hand."

Psalm 71:19-21

"For thy righteousness, O God, reaches to the heavens, thou has done great things; O God, who is like Thee? Thou, who has shown me many troubles and distresses, wilt revive me again, and wilt bring me up again from the depths of the earth. Mayest Thou increase my greatness, and turn to comfort me."

APPENDIX II

SCRIPTURE MEMORY

Isaiah 55:11 is a **PROMISE** that God's Word will not return void. We have used an acrostic of the word "promise" as a helpful guideline for Scripture memory.

Pray

Pray about what the Lord would have you memorize. Begin with verses that have special meaning for you from this book. Set realistic goals for yourself about how many verses to memorize each week and work on it daily. Eventually you may want to memorize a whole chapter or even a whole book of the Bible.

Repetition

Repetition is the key to effective scripture memory. Read each verse until you can repeat it without looking. Try repeating verses out loud – it will use another one of your senses. When you have memorized a verse add a new verse to what you have memorized. If you miss a day or two, start where you left off.

Organize

Use 3x5 index cards. Example: Psalm 139 has 24 verses: use 3 index cards and put 8 verses on the card-4 verses on the front and 4 on the back. Make sure you proofread each verse that you have written on your index cards.

Meditate

Meditate on the words in each verse to understand its meaning and apply it to your life. Repeat the verse slowly emphasizing a different word each time. Look up words to clarify their meaning. Ask yourself what does this say about God and how can I use it in my life? Be sure you understand the context's effect on the interpretation.

Inspire

Inspire others by sharing what you are doing. It would help you to be accountable to a person in your church or a family member. Repeat verses to them when you meet. Be encouraging!

Saturate

Saturate your mind with God's Word so it can renew your thinking and you may grow in godly wisdom.

Edify

Edification is to be the purpose of our speech (Ephesians 4:29). As God's Word becomes a part of your life, your edifying words will flow from your renewed mind and bring glory to God in your witness for Him. Trust me, Scripture memory will effectively transform your life.

You may want to start on a few verses that we have listed throughout this book to help you grow stronger in your relationship with the Lord Jesus.

Appendix III

A Few Words From My Husband

Dear Reader,

As a husband, pastor, and biblical counselor I understand the pain you are experiencing as you struggle with infertility or the loss of a child through miscarriage, stillbirth, or an early infant death. I am sorry for your loss and grieve with you. I also want you to know that God is working out His perfect plan for your life. The Apostle Paul boasted in God's perfecting work when he wrote, *"[For I am] confident of this very thing, that He who began a good work in you will perfect it until the day of Christ Jesus"* (Philippians 1:6). That's God's promise to you!

The pain is deep and the road is long that leads you to peace and the understanding of God's sovereign plan for you and your family. Yet God's grace is sufficient to strengthen you every minute of every dark day until you begin to see the light on His path.

I know your pain because I have walked through these same purifying flames with my wife, Sandy. I thanked the Lord again this morning for using Sandy and me through the loss of our son Caleb to minister His comfort to others like you. It is such a privilege to serve God together as a couple to help you. As you read the book and weep and grow, please don't hesitate to contact us and allow us the opportunity to walk this road along with you.

Finally, remember God wants to use your life to glorify Him and a great way to do that is to share your struggles with someone else. In time, allow God to use your life's pain to help others who suffer. Permit them to experience the comfort you have received from God.

"Blessed [be] the God and Father of our Lord Jesus Christ, the Father of mercies and God of all comfort; who comforts us in all our affliction so that we may be able to comfort those who are in any affliction with the comfort with which we ourselves are comforted by God" (2 Corinthians 1:3-4).

For the love, mercy, and grace of God,

Craig Day, M.Div.
Founder/Ministry Development
Caleb Ministries

APPENDIX IV

CALEB HISTORY

Over the years, our volunteers have been blessed to watch as God comforts and restores broken and hurting women through Caleb Ministries as well as its Outreach Ministries. It has been a journey orchestrated by God.

On Sunday August 5, 1990, sitting in the choir loft of her church, Sandy realized that God wanted her to comfort others in their loss with the comfort she had received from God. Her heart ached to share God's comfort with women like herself who had suffered deep, painful losses. In 1988 Craig and Sandy had experienced God's comfort during the loss of their precious son, Caleb. In the days that followed, they gave prayerful consideration to the organization of a ministry for others who were experiencing sorrow. That ministry would be named in memory of their much loved and missed son.

In the early days of Caleb Ministries, Sandy had many opportunities to travel and share her testimony of God's comfort through His Word. Sandy's transparent truthfulness about her struggles impacted the lives of countless women who have attended these conferences and retreats.

After only one year of ministry, Caleb Ministries expanded to include a personal one-on-one ministry to women who had experienced miscarriage, stillbirth, early infant death or infertility. The story of Caleb in Numbers 13 and 14 from which the name Caleb Cares emerged, provided insight for this ministry to the sorrowing. It was at this time that Caleb Ministries became a 501(c)(3) non-profit Christian organization.

Even as Sandy was ministering to other women, God continued His convicting work in her life. Through His Word, God showed her that in order to minister to others, she would have to allow every area of her life to be exposed to the light of His truth. God continually exposed hidden areas that required her repentant confession in her growing walk with God. As she responded to God's refining fire, the ministry grew with her.

One of the outgrowths of this responsiveness to God was a prayer journal called **In Everything By Prayer** that Sandy developed with her friend Donna Peters. Through the years, God has used this unique tool to encourage women to have a more consistent prayer life. With over 15,000 copies of the journal in print, many families have been blessed. The most popular section of the journal entitled "How to pray for your Husband/ Children," has helped many women support their families with effective prayer.

In 1993, two years into the ministry of Caleb Cares, Sandy compiled nine stories of individuals who had experienced the loss of a child and received God's restoring grace into the book entitled **Morning Will Come**. Volunteers scanned the obituaries of local papers and sent copies of the book to women who had lost children. The response was overwhelming. With 10,000 copies in print, letters came from women around the world with testimony to the encouragement it had brought to them.

Caleb Cares chapters began forming across the U.S. by 1995. Each chapter began by providing copies of **Morning Will Come** to hurting women in their areas. It was also during this time that a Caleb Ministries Women's Discipleship Retreat was organized. Each year since then women attend from all over the country to hear outstanding Bible teaching and find encouragement. It never fails to be a time of spiritual renewal for all who attend.

In the summer of 1995, God brought still another dimension to Caleb Ministries. God led nine women to call the ministry who had lost babies, each indicating that they had experienced a prior abortion. As Sandy ministered to these women she realized God wanted to use her own abortion, at age 19, to help other women. In response to God's conviction, Sandy confessed her abortion to her father, opening the door for complete family restoration. Through this difficult time, God prepared Sandy to talk publicly about the short and long-term effects of abortion. Her story exposes long held secrets and touches those who hear of the forgiving power of God.

A second manuscript used by Caleb Ministries was completed in 1998. The devotional journal, **The Memories I Cherish**, was developed by Sandy Day together with Donna Elyea. This beautifully presented keepsake provides a place to record the journey of one's walk with God through their time of loss. It serves to help them remember the comfort and encouragement they received in the years to come.

The P.A.T. (Providing A Treasure) Ministry began with a passion to assist a grieving woman or couple in a loving, yet practical way. The P.A.T. box includes a burial gown, bonnet, blanket, as well as a Caleb Cares brochure, an envelope to hold a lock of the baby's hair, and a copy of **Morning Will Come** or a new booklet dealing specifically with stillbirth or early infant death. These items are wrapped in acid-free tissue paper and tucked in a precious box that parents will treasure through the years. P.A.T. boxes are provided to hospitals and funeral homes across the US, and make their way into the arms of those who tragically have no child to bring home. The boxes are also available by individual request.

Abbey's Place, our post-abortion ministry, got underway in 1999. Its goal is to provide support and guidance to women who are struggling with the guilt, pain, and grief of a past abortion decision. Our hope is that each person God sends to us will achieve spiritual and emotional restoration through Christ. Toward that end, a third book was written to minister particularly to this growing segment of the population. The book, **Living in His Forgiveness**, presents stories of men and women who have successfully moved past their pain to find freedom from their guilt in Christ's forgiveness. A Bible study is included to guide the seeking heart to discover God's redeeming truth.

In January of 2000, Craig Day followed his call to seminary, moving with his family to California. The ministry continually grew by leaps and bounds as a West Coast Chapter began and a Caleb Ministries web site was constructed in order to make materials and contact information available to women everywhere. It is a blessing to see God use technology to distribute much-needed assistance on-line! Craig graduated in May 2002 and is now pastoring a church in Charlotte, NC.

Caleb Chapters continue to form in other states, as God raises up godly leaders in local churches with a vision to minister to those weighed down by grief or guilt. We stand amazed at the way God burdens women to minister to women, and at the way He intervenes to make all things possible.

Since its beginnings in 1990, Caleb Ministries has flourished as God has led us as individuals, as chapters, and as an international ministry. Faithful men and women, hand-picked by the Father, serve as Board of Directors, ministry coordinators, and volunteers. We count it a privilege to continually help women who are struggling with difficult seasons and situations and to nurture them in the ways of the Lord – the only One who can truly help and heal.

APPENDIX V

HOW WE MINISTER

The Mission of Caleb Ministries is to reach people with the gospel of Jesus Christ and to establish them in right relationship with Him, according to the Word of God, through compassionate outreach, teaching, biblical counsel, and discipleship.

Ministry Outreaches:

Sandy Day's Speaking Ministry

Sandy Day is an exciting speaker with a ministering heart. God uses her to draw people to Christ because of her love for God's Word and her desire for others to be helped by it. Sandy's enthusiasm for Christ is contagious – her love for Jesus abounds. Sandy and her husband Craig are the Founders of Caleb Ministries. She is available for speaking engagements/women's conferences. Her testimony, "Who Wrote This Story" is available on cassette.

Caleb Cares

This outreach ministry provides support and encouragement to women who are struggling with the trauma of infertility, miscarriage, stillbirth, and early infant death. Volunteers who have suffered similar experiences are paired one-on-one with clients. They offer the compassion of a friend who understands grief and the comfort that Jesus Christ provides through His Word. Couples Bible studies are offered as well as women's Bible studies for those who have lost a baby. Also, Caleb Chapters have been formed across the U.S. If you would like to inquire about a chapter or are interested in starting one in your city, please e-mail the ministry at info@calebministries.org and guidelines will be sent to you.

The P.A.T. Ministry (Providing A Treasure)

This outreach ministry provides beautiful memorial boxes to women who have experienced a stillbirth or early infant death. The boxes contain a burial gown, a blanket, a bonnet, an envelope for the baby's hair, and a copy of "Morning Will Come" or a grief booklet. They may be kept and used as a treasure box for the baby's memorabilia. They are distributed to churches, hospitals, and doctors' offices, as well as by direct request.

Abbey's Place

This outreach ministry provides support and guidance to women who are struggling with the guilt, pain, and grief of an abortion decision. Volunteers who have suffered through the same traumatic decision are paired one-on-one with clients. Small group Bible studies are also offered.

Women's Discipleship Retreats

Every fall women gather from across the U.S. to hear God's relevant Word and share warm fellowship at our life-changing Women's Discipleship Retreats at Springmaid Beach, SC (South Myrtle Beach). The purposes of our retreats are to firmly root, build up, and establish Christian women in the truth of God's Word (Colossians 2:6-7). Call our ministry for this year's brochure. You will be blessed!

APPENDIX VI

WE CARE FOR YOU

A PERSONAL WORD

Dear Reader,

We hope you have been encouraged and comforted by reading about the struggles and victories of others who have gone through difficulties that you have experienced or may be experiencing now in your life.

Woven throughout these stories is the message of hope and peace that came as each one developed a deeper relationship with Jesus Christ. Often we find that God uses the hard times in our lives to draw us close to Him and His Son.

Accepting Christ into your life and walking with Him is as simple as "confessing with your mouth the Lord Jesus, and believing that God raised Him from the dead, and you shall be saved" (Romans 10:9). That simple commitment promises us eternal life and a Savior who is the same yesterday, today, and forever (Hebrews 13:8).

If you have made a commitment to Jesus Christ and would like further information about being a Christian, please write and we'll send materials to you.

God Bless You,

Sandy Day

 ANY QUESTIONS?

Would you like a newsletter or could we be of any help to you?
Call or e-mail us: 1-877-4U-CALEB – info@calebministries.org
Visit our secured website at www.calebministries.org. for online ordering.

TO CONTACT US:

Sandy Day
C/O Caleb Ministries
PO Box 470093
Charlotte, NC 28247
1-877-4U-CALEB OR (704) 841-1320

Sandy is available for Women's Conferences and Retreats. Visit our website at www.calebministries.org. Email us at: info@calebministries.org for additional help or information.

Also, every fall Caleb Ministries has a Women's Discipleship Retreat at Springmaid Beach, SC (South Myrtle Beach, SC). E-mail us at retreat@calebministries.org for this year's brochure.